THE APOSTOLIC PROPHETIC HEART OF GOD

THE APOSTOLIC PROPHETIC HEART OF GOD

Seen in Fatherhood & Sonship, the Divine Pattern for Restoration!

PATRICK M. O'NEAL

HAM Intl Books

Copyright © 2023 Patrick M. O'Neal

All rights reserved. No part of this book may be reproduced in any manner whatsoever without written permission except in the case of brief quotations embodied in critical articles and reviews.

First Printing, 2023 in Australia by HAM Intl Books

National Library of Australia Cataloguing-in-Publication entry

Creator: O'Neal, Patrick M., author.

Title: The Apostolic Prophetic Heart of God:
Seen in Fatherhood and Sonship, The Divine Pattern for Restoration! / Patrick M. O'Neal.

ISBN 9780645735628 (Paperback)

Practical Theology/Christian Life; experience; & practice/Christian living

Dewey Number: 248

**All Scriptures taken from the New King James Version® Copyright © 1982 by Thomas Nelson.
Used by permission. All rights reserved.**

Italics with no quotation marks are done by the author for the purpose of emphasis.

Italics within quotation marks are direct scriptures quotes or portions of scripture quotes from New King James Version® Copyright © 1982 by Thomas Nelson.

Bold Italics within quotations marks are direct scripture quotes or portions of direct scripture quotes from the New King James Version® Copyright © 1982 by Thomas Nelson are done by the author for the purpose of emphasis.

I Dedicate this Book:

To my Heavenly Father
who chose me, called me and saved me through Christ's supreme and loving sacrifice at Calvary and saw fit to consider me faithful, putting me into the apostolic ministry!

To my beloved wife Diane (nee Salvatico) O'Neal
I am eternally grateful to God for such a Help-mate as you. The one who has endlessly prayed for me and encouraged me to write and publish this work. The one who has faithfully stood beside me and with me, as closest companion, best friend, counsellor and confidant through so many of life's challenges.

To my great grandparents Ps Albert and Mrs Mary Lowe
who paved the way with their prayers for the generations to come by leaving a great spiritual legacy and impacting my life, even without ever meeting face to face! We will meet in glory!

To my grandmother Ruth (nee Lowe) O'Neal
who sat and learned at Smith Wigglesworth's feet. Nana you were always such a great example of Christ's love in my life at all times. Your constant encouragement and reminders continually stirred me up in the faith. Your undying love and passion to share the gospel was contagious and spurred me on. Saying farewell to you was so hard and yet cause for great rejoicing. Enjoy your eternal home Nana!

To my father Charles Robert O'Neal
who rescued me from the flames! Who worked hard and tirelessly gave in practical instruction and training as a son, to help me reach manhood and eventually become a father.

To my mother Marilyn Joan (nee Walmsley) O'Neal
who sacrificed all to nurture me, even from before I was born, right through to manhood. Who helped me to understand and recognise the value of a woman as a mother, wife and so much more.

To my spiritual father Paul Evans
who discipled me and helped me as a spiritual babe in Christ. Teaching me great discernment, and helping me to get established with a solid foundation in the Christian faith.

To Rev Gordon Broussard a spiritual father
who trained me in the ministry in the early years, teaching me the importance of self-discipline, courage and determination in reaching the lost!

To my father in the faith & ministry Rev John Wilkinson.
A man who sat and learned under Smith Wigglesworth's ministry. You were a great father and apostolic example to me: who demonstrated and taught me so much about walking with God and being sustained by God's grace in the ministry, through intimacy, integrity, accountability, responsibility & authority.

I love and honour you all and say thank you for your contribution to my life!

Patrick M. O'Neal

A THANK YOU

As the author, let me start out by saying a big *thank you*, to *you* the reader, for wanting to take the time out of your busy schedule to read this book.

Books take much time to write, and much time to read. If there was no one willing to read a book, there would be no need to write a book.

Much information, inspiration, impartation and understanding comes, with writing and reading books. So again, thank you for taking the time.

To help with the readers background knowledge & understanding of the author, I would like It made known that it is the author's position, that the Holy Bible which is referred to many times through out this publication, is the authoritative, inspired, infallible and unchanging Word of God!

It is also the authors belief and conviction that, the life changing message of salvation for all of humanity, is found in the gospel and person of Jesus Christ, which is written within the pages of the Holy Bible!

John 3:16
"For God so loved the world that He gave His only begotten Son, that whoever believes in Him should not perish but have everlasting life."

A NOTE ABOUT WORDS

The author's use of the words *'Son', 'Sons', 'Father', 'Fathers'*, is intended to be inclusive of the masculine and the feminine!

The term *'Son'* is also inclusive of the term *'Daughter'* which is equally so, with the term *'Sons'* being inclusive of the term *'Daughters'*.

The same can be said for the terms *'Father/Mother'* & *'Fathers/Mothers'*.

In some parts of the book, the author has tried to use both the masculine and feminine terms together. In other places it is too cumbersome.

According to ancient custom the terms *'Son'* or *'Sons'* as used in the Bible, was a term which could also sometimes be applied, to the feminine as well as the masculine, except for literal translation and meaning when found in certain contexts.

For example: when the Holy Bible talks about *'the revealing of the Sons of God'* it includes the feminine as well as the masculine.

It is not the authors intention to offend, upset or leave anyone out. What is written in this book is meant to be taken as all inclusive!

It is the author's prayer that as you read this book, you are blessed with a revelation of *who you are in Him*!

A PRAYER OF BLESSING

Numbers 6:24-26

²⁴ "The Lord bless you and keep you;
²⁵ The Lord make His face shine upon you,
And be gracious to you;
²⁶ The Lord lift up His countenance upon you,
And give you peace."

Amen!

CONTENTS

Copyright — iv
Dedication — v
A Thank You — ix
A Note About Words — xi
A Prayer of Blessing — xiii

One
An Introduction and Understanding! — 1

Two
A Heart Restored and Remade! — 9

Three
A Father and Two Sons! — 16

Four
Becoming a Father! — 30

Five
The Revealing of the Sons of God! — 37

Six
Character Qualities found in a Spiritual Son or Daughter! — 45

Seven
Restoring the Revelation! — 51

Eight
Restoration Based on the Everlasting Covenant! — 62

Nine
The Restoration of Foundations and a Cutting Edge! — 69

Ten
Restoration of Inheritance, Gifts and Callings! — 80

Eleven
Restoration of Unity and Grace! — 90

Twelve
Restoration of the Soul! — 103

Thirteen
Restoring the Soul and Diagram! — 109

Fourteen
Restoration of All Things List & Flow Chart! — 123

Fifteen
Conclusion to the Apostolic Prophetic Heart of God! — 129

Sixteen
Family History and Spiritual Heritage! — 133

About the Author — 145
Future Publications — 149

CHAPTER ONE

An Introduction and Understanding!

In this present day, many are struggling to understand the apostolic and prophetic gifts and callings of God. We need to understand that the order and timing for the restoration of these two foundational ministry gifts, has been in focus on God's time clock, since the mid to late 1980's.

There are so many factors that influence our understanding. The streams of the Holy Spirit that you have been swimming in, and the Christian doctrine you have been yoked to, in whichever branch of the Church you have been part of, will contribute to and shape your views. Alongside that, is the culture and geographical location you have lived and served in.

Over the last 30-40 years in particular, the function and role of the apostle and prophet have often been misunderstood and abused in use and, or acceptance in the Church! Some treat these gifts with suspicion, some treat them with contempt and others just aren't sure. Many have picked up and run with the terms *apostle* and *prophet* like they are meant to be solely used as titles. There has been little or no correct understanding of their function and purpose. Therefore an inability to recognise these gifts of Christ, given to the Church.

A lot of emphasis in some churches, denominations and groups has been placed on status, celebrity, perceived authority and a total neglect of the importance of relationship and connection with the other ministry gifts and members of the body of Christ.

Some apostles and prophets will identify as apostles and prophets of a denomination, and still others will identify as apostles and prophets of Jesus Christ! Needless to say that, such gifts (If they are true gifts) are given to the family of God by Christ. I will leave you the reader to decide which is correct!

Many times we have looked at what they do in their roles and functions and tried to understand them; rather than what they are, that is to say what an apostle and prophet is really like in heart and character! The apostolic prophetic heart should reveal itself as *being one with* and just *like* the Father. As Jesus himself has said; in the gospel of Luke 6:44 *"for every tree is known by its own fruit"*.

In Proverbs 4:23 we are told that the issues of life flow from the heart. Therefore we need to look upon the heart of the individual who is before us, just as the prophet Samuel was instructed to do by God, when he was sent to search out and anoint David as king of Israel (1 Samuel 16:7,12).

Sometimes it's easier to understand the role and function of a ministry gift by looking at its effects and results; which is part of what this book is about. Having said that; one must also discern according to the word of God and by the Holy Spirit what is a genuine; from what is a counterfeit ministry gift.

This is where we can take a *leaf* out of the apostle Paul's book (proverbially speaking) when he says in 1 Corinthians 11:19 *"For there must also be factions among you, that those who are approved may be recognized among you."* I like to call this: *'the law of contrast'* principle. Like the colors black and white which are known and recognized by their contrasting difference.

In this season the apostolic and prophetic anointing of the Holy Spirit, is being given by God to His apostles and prophets, to provide the necessary fathering to those He is raising up and releasing as the true sons and daughters of God. The anointing that is upon the fathers, imparts what is needed for resilience, growth and maturity to be brought forth in the sons and daughters of God.

The apostolic prophetic heart is the Father's heart. It restores Fatherhood, Sonship, Relationship and Family. True sons, are produced by true fathers. True sons, are ultimately to become fathers.

In this brief publication, I would like to focus on the results and the effects of the heart, the character, and the function of these two, all important, indispensable ministry gifts. It is necessary to get a fuller understanding and to also fully appreciate their place in the body of Christ, according to the way in which the Spirit of God is working in these latter days.

The reality is; that without the apostolic prophetic heart of God in those chosen to function in the gift of apostle and prophet, there can be no fuller maturity brought to the body of Christ. Neither can there be a proper equipping, training and sending and therefore; neither can there be a successful advancement of the kingdom of God and fruitful effective evangelization of the world!

Jesus has told us to go into all the world and preach the gospel. He said, make disciples and baptize them in the name of the Father, Son and Holy Spirit. He has told us to teach them to observe all these things He has taught us. Jesus has also told us that upon *"this Rock I will build My Church"*, that is the *confession* based on a *revelation* given by the Father that says... *'thou art the Christ the Son of the Living God'*. This is a revelation given to those whose hearts are sincere, and in the right position to receive it.

That revelation of Christ must first be restored to the Church and then to the unsaved person who finds Christ as their Saviour and Lord. Apostles and prophets are the ones that are being raised by the Father and given the heart and motivation to bring this to bear on the Church and the world. They have a desire for the holiness and purity of Christ, to be restored to the Church. They have a God given desire and purity of heart to see this brought to bear on the world through the Church.

The apostolic prophetic heart also pushes to see the restoration of all things unto God through Christ. The call is big. The grace given by Jesus to His chosen apostles and prophets is sufficient. The hearts of His servants are being made ready through trial, testing, tribulation, rejection, bitter experience, discipline, holiness and of course an intimacy of relationship that allows them to hear and receive from Jesus Christ and in turn impact the Church and the world.

In Matthew 3:11 we are told that *"Jesus will baptize with the Holy Spirit & fire"* One has to wonder what might have happened; if we had allowed ourselves to be subjected to His Spirit and fire much sooner in modern church history. Maybe we would have seen more of His holy apostles and prophets released & sent forth earlier on His time clock?.....One wonders!

Up until the time I wrote the teaching that follows in this book, I had been through so much of the questioning and seeking process that one goes through in counting the cost, to follow Jesus according to the apostolic call. I wouldn't for many years; even remotely mention the fact that I was called to serve as an apostle! The body of Christ at least in my part of the world at the time, was not at all accepting of the idea, that anyone could be called as an apostle, especially at the age I was back then.

Those of a doctrinal point of view that is *cessational* or even *dispensational*, would not accept the restoration of such gifts and callings to the Church at all. Then there are many others who don't recognise that they have ever existed. Some of those same individuals also don't accept the manifestation and operation of the gifts of the Holy Spirit.

I discovered over time as I continued my walk with Jesus; that ignoring the apostolic call on my life, wasn't going to make it go away. Actually it just intensified the call a whole lot more. Over the course of time I have realised, that my experiences, training and relationships with other men and women of God as leaders in the body of Christ, has propelled me all the more; towards my apostolic prophetic call!

At the beginning of the 1990's I was directed by the Lord Jesus to go on an extended period of fasting. During that time of fasting, I struggled and questioned the Lord about many things. I asked one thing of the lord in particular. I said *"Lord, please give me a spiritual father"*. One who has decades of ministry experience, but more importantly decades of walking with the Lord. I also specifically requested of the Lord, that He give me a spiritual father that walked with a limp.

God answered my prayer in every detail. At the time I had been doing a character study on the life of Jacob. Jacob was the one who wrestled with God and was left with a mark, walked with a limp, and had his name changed, representing a changed character and heart (Genesis 32:22-32).

When I first met the man God gave me to be my spiritual father and mentor for the next 3 years, I was surprised and almost shocked. I showed up in a suit and tie with well polished shoes. He greeted me at the door with a big smile a warm hand shake and also dressed in like manner. He invited me in and gave me a task. He said to me "I want you to go and sweep out the back room of the Church building" I thought to myself, I didn't come here for that. He handed me a broom (I didn't argue or question him) I accepted it, took off my jacket, rolled up my shirt sleeves and started sweeping. Next thing I realised, he was right there alongside me, also with a broom and also sweeping! Here was the 75 year old man, that God had given me as a spiritual father, with more than 50 years ministry experience. He was dressed in a suit and tie, jacket off, sleeves rolled up and sweeping a dusty, dirty storage room.

This experience humbled me so much. But his example was the most humbling thing for me. The fact that he got in there with me and led by example. It wasn't beneath him. He didn't have a problem with pride. It was a great test for me and a great demonstration of apostolic grace from a father in the faith.

As I look back now over the past few decades of my life, I can see God's preparation and finger prints everywhere. His affirmations, confirmations, rebukes, corrections, instructions and His loving care and guidance can be seen all over. Everything from divine appointments, to people I served under in all the different ministry functions and roles. It was training, training and more training! Training in character, training in spirit. Training in development of a pure and healthy heart. Training in ministry skills. Training as a *Son* not just as a *Servant*.

Learning to become a *son* in *heart* has been important and instrumental in preparing me to become a spiritual father to so many. I continue to learn and grow with every spiritual son and daughter that God gives me as a father. It is always another opportunity for more lessons to be learned. The father's heart proceeds out of the heart of a son, which is why they tell me allegorically, *"old wine is sweeter and more mellow than new wine"*. You can always identify a son who has a spiritual father. It is evident in the fruit.

Jesus puts it aptly when He says to to Phillip in John 14:8-11 *"He who has seen Me has seen the Father"* in the same passage Jesus says *"Believe Me when I say that I am in the Father and the father is in Me...."*

Apostles and prophets must eventually become as fathers and mothers spiritually! This is what the body of Christ needs today, not managers and CEO's. Apostles and prophets are given the keys to divine patterns and solutions! As apostle Paul said in Acts 26:19 *"I was not disobedient to the heavenly vision."* Fatherhood and sonship is the divine pattern for restoration today, just as it was back when Paul and Timothy walked the dusty roads of Asia Minor.

Wisdom, grace, humility and being teachable were some of the keys to the early apostles' journey with Jesus. The qualities of courage, trust, faithfulness, righteousness, purity and a steadfastness of heart were instilled in them, the more they journeyed with Jesus. To learn from Jesus they had to truly become, not only as disciples, but as sons learning everything there is to learn from a father that embraces them in their every lesson.

First being a true and committed disciple is what led to them being selected and appointed as the first apostles. First learning to become as a son recognising that the father was in Jesus, is what led to them becoming not only apostles, but also becoming as fathers to the early church.

Apostles along with prophets are truly the *sent ones*. They are sent at the word of Jesus command, spoken in the ear and whispered in the heart of the one who listens! They sit at His feet and they hear His word. They are sent out of the presence of the King of kings Jesus Christ, on a mission to turn the world right side up!

They work to build the Father's House! They seek to restore to God what is rightfully His; as paid for and redeemed by the blood of His Son Jesus. They have a heart to see the work of restoration take place in body, soul and spirit. They have a passion to raise the sons and daughters of God.

1 Corinthians 4:15 *"For though you might have ten thousand instructors in Christ, yet you do not have many fathers; for in Christ Jesus I have begotten you through the gospel."*

I say "Thank you Father God for all the instructors you have given me over the years to teach me . More importantly Heavenly Father, I thank you for the few real spiritual fathers that I have had the privilege of being trained and mentored by."

There is more I could say here in this opening chapter, but as with all truth that God reveals, it continues to grow as it is unpacked. I will leave it at this point and allow you to continue to read what God has allowed me to write.

***

Ephesians 4:11-16

"[11] *And* **He Himself gave** *some to be* **apostles**, *some* **prophets**, *some evangelists, and some pastors and teachers,* [12] *for the equipping of the saints for the work of ministry, for the edifying of the body of Christ,* [13] *till we all come to the unity of the faith and of the knowledge of the Son of God, to a perfect man, to the measure of the stature of the fullness of Christ;* [14] *that we should no longer be children, tossed to and fro and carried about with every wind of doctrine, by the trickery of men, in the cunning craftiness of deceitful plotting,* [15] *but, speaking the truth in love,* **may grow up in all things into Him who is the head— Christ—***"*

***

CHAPTER TWO

A Heart Restored and Remade!

Restored hearts bring restoration! A restored heart is a new heart. The Father gives a new heart to those who repent and put their faith and trust in His only begotten Son Jesus Christ. A heart of restoration that can only come through the remission of sins, because of the shed blood of Jesus, on the cross at Calvary.

The heart is at the centre of everything in our lives, that we feel, say and do! Our hearts can motivate or de-motivate. Our heart can pollute and bring division in the lives of others as well as our own life. Our heart can be caught in double-mindedness and remain fragmented, or be united by the *Word and the Spirit*. Our heart can betray and lead us astray, or lift us to the mountain tops, bringing great strength & encouragement to us, in the love and purpose of God!

The writer of Psalm 119:11 says *"Your word I have hidden in my heart, that I might not sin against You."* It was Jeremiah who stated in Jeremiah 17:9-10 *"The heart is deceitful above all things, and desperately wicked; who can know it? [10]I, the Lord, search the heart, I test the mind, even to give every man according to his ways, according to the fruit of his doings"*

It was David who declared in Psalm 73:26 *"My flesh and my heart fail; but God is the strength of my heart and my portion forever."*

David's statement highlights the fact that, the heart is central. But He knew that God must be its strength and portion! With no anchor our hearts become restless and disturbed so easily, like a ship tossed too and fro, in a rough sea.

Psalm 34:18 *says "The Lord is near to those who have a broken heart, And saves such as have a contrite spirit."* A broken heart is the condition of many who can't seem to embrace a dream or a vision for their future. This of course God knows, and He deliberately draws near waiting for a cry that shows a readiness, to embrace Him in all his fullness. Hence the writer of Proverbs 4:23 says *"Keep your heart with all diligence, for out of it spring the issues of life."*

Yet again let us consider: Proverbs 17:22 *"A merry heart does good, like medicine, but a broken spirit dries the bones."*

Sometimes the only remedy is heart surgery of the *Divine* kind. The prophet Ezekiel tells us that God would give us a new heart and put a new spirit within us, as a part of His restorative work. That He would deal with the stony, hard heart and give us a soft heart, a heart of flesh.

Ezekiel 36:26-27 *"²⁶I will give you a new heart and put a new spirit within you; I will take the heart of stone out of your flesh and give you a heart of flesh. ²⁷I will put My Spirit within you and cause you to walk in My statutes, and you will keep My judgments and do them."*

And yet again the prophet Jeremiah says in....Jeremiah 31:33 *"But this is the covenant that I will make with the house of Israel after those days, says the Lord: I will put My law in their minds, and write it* **on their hearts;** *and I will be their God, and they shall be My people."*

Hebrews 10:16 *"This is the covenant that I will make with them after those days, says the Lord: I will put My laws **into their hearts,** and in their minds I will write them,"*

Jesus the only begotten son of God, declared the thought, intent and purpose of His Father on the sabbath, when He stood up and read boldly from the prophet Isaiah in the synagogue in Nazareth. In so doing he revealed the Father's restorative heart.

He had been baptised by His cousin John the Baptist and filled with the Holy Spirit at the river Jordan (Luke 3:21-22). His time of testing in the wilderness had ended (Luke 4:1-13), when He emphasised the healing of the broken hearted and being set free from every other associated ailment of the human heart and soul.

Luke 4:18-19 *"The Spirit of the Lord is upon Me, because He has anointed Me to preach the gospel to the poor; He has sent Me to heal the brokenhearted, to proclaim liberty to the captives and recovery of sight to the blind, to set at liberty those who are oppressed; ¹⁹To proclaim the acceptable year of the Lord."*

A heart of restoration can be found in the apostolic prophetic heart, that God is giving increasingly, to His holy apostles and prophets as He restores them to the church, and to the work of extending the kingdom of God on earth. Our hearts must become as the heart of Christ, that is: compassionate, wise, discerning and as gentle as a dove!

WHAT DOES RESTORATION MEAN? Biblically speaking, restoration means to make restitution. It carries with it the idea of making something whole and complete again. To make up for what lacks. To heal or mend that which is broken, damaged or wounded. To bring something back to original condition.

There is a discernible shift and change towards restoration taking place in the *body of Christ, the Church* today. It can be seen in the following four areas as a **shift and a change towards:**

1. RELATIONSHIP - Intimacy, face to face and heart to heart.

2. FAMILY - fathers, mothers, children in the natural and spiritual.

3. FATHERHOOD - parenting in the natural and spiritual.

4. SON-SHIP - identity, training, equipping, inheritance

For this to happen, God is giving to many a:

1. NEW HEART - the Father's heart Ezekiel 36:26 and with it a

2. NEW ANOINTING - Father's blessing and anointing. Fresh Oil Psalm 92:10 which brings with it a

3. NEW EQUIPPING - Ps 144:1 hands are trained for war and fingers for battle, which makes way for a

4. NEW MANTLE - and being clothed, endued with power from on high, like putting on a new cloak or covering. Joel 2: 28-29, Acts 1:8, Luke 24: 49, 2 Kings 2:13-15.

MANY ARE BEING REMADE!

God will make of an individual and do with an individual what suits Him and His Purpose; not ours. This principle can be seen in the account of Jeremiah 18:1-17 (v3-v6) where he is told to go down to the potters house that he might hear what God would say to him concerning Israel and being likened to a clay vessel that was marred and needed to be remade on the potters wheel. Verse 4 says, *"so he made it again"* (see also Hebrews 13: 21) The Potter is of course equivalent to the Father (God), that disciplines, corrects, fashions and shapes His sons & daughters.

I remember back in the month of April 2000, receiving a phone call from a lady at around 6.30am in the morning. I will never forget her words. She said *"God has told me to tell you that you are going back on the potter's wheel"*. Then she immediately hung up. I stood there with the phone still in my hand, and those words ringing in my ears and resonating in my mind and heart. I knew God had spoken to me and I had to be ready. This word pierced my heart as it came at a time of extreme heartache and crisis in my life. It was inescapable. If I was going to survive and make it through God's remaking, then I had to hang on to Him with every fibre of my being.

My whole world literally fell apart. But God was remaking me. I surrendered every ministry responsibility I had at that time. I was in a time and season when many doors had been opened to me. I had just planted another new fellowship and was training new leaders. I was speaking into the foundations of young churches. By divine appointment; God was taking me places in his purposes. Even some of the fellowships that God had me ministering to, were cross cultural and so I found myself speaking and prophesying by the Spirit in other languages in some of those churches. The *dying to self* that I had to do, was painful. I had to surrender it all. I was being remade.

I remember approximately 3 months after the phone call, standing in my lounge room where I was living at the time, with tears running down my face; and hands raised saying to Father God *"I will do what you want me to do Lord and serve you no matter what it costs me, I surrender it all to you Lord, I Love you Lord, do what you want with me"*. I had to acknowledge that God was remaking me. *Many of us are being remade* The way we minister and serve should reflect this discernible shift & change in restoration.

As *the Father* gives new hearts we see him restoring apostles and prophets back to *the Church*. The restorative heart of God is seen through the apostles and prophets. The restorative heart is the Father's heart. The restorative heart is a heart of 1. Grace and 2. Faith. Grace and Faith is what it takes to empower, equip & release members of God's family for service.

God the Father is bringing about the *restoration of all things* to Himself. Even as He restores all things to Himself, we will see His glory cover the earth as the waters cover the sea. As it says in Habakkuk 2:14 *"For the earth will be filled with the knowledge of the glory of the Lord, as the waters cover the sea."*

Isaiah 60:1 says *"Arise, shine; for your light has come! And the glory of the Lord is risen upon you."* His manifest Glory will be seen on the sons and daughters of God, more and more, as they are revealed.

Acts 3:21 say's concerning Jesus God's Son *"whom heaven must receive until the restoration of all things, which God has spoken by the mouth of all his holy prophets since the world began."*

Jesus is being held back in heaven, seated at the right hand of the Father, interceding for us, awaiting the restoration of all things! The Father is making preparations for the revealing of the sons of God and for the sending of His glorified exalted Son Jesus Christ, according to the fullness of time and the fulfillment of His word, spoken by His prophets.

Let us pray ...Loving and Holy God, The God and Father of our Lord Jesus Christ, may the restoration of all things not be delayed, and may the sons and daughters of God be made ready for your return. Heavenly Father, Lord Jesus Christ, Holy Spirit, let your glory cover the earth as the waters cover the sea. Let your glory arise upon us Lord. Let your light shine in and through us, into the darkest of places. Amen!

****
Romans 8:18
*"For I consider that the sufferings of this present time are not worthy to be compared with **the glory which shall be revealed in us.**"*
****

CHAPTER THREE

A Father and Two Sons!

Luke 15:1-3 *"Then all the tax collectors and the sinners drew near to Him to hear Him. ²And the Pharisees and scribes complained, saying, "This Man receives sinners and eats with them." ³So He spoke this parable to them, saying:....."* (& v4-v32)

Jesus, after being followed by the multitudes, and speaking to them about the cost of being a disciple, proceeds to share a parable with tax collectors and sinners! The story focuses on a *lost sheep*, a *lost coin*, and a *lost son*. The lesson to be learned is singular in its focus and conclusion but reinforced three times over! Jesus now has the attention of the tax collectors and other sinners. He also has Pharisees and scribes listening in and complaining about him rubbing shoulders with the lesser citizens of society.

This parable epitomises the apostolic prophetic heart of Father God. The Fathers heart towards those that He comes to seek and save! Luke 19:10 says *"for the Son of Man has come to seek and save that which was lost."* But not only to seek and save, but also to make *Sons* of them.

In the Father's eyes, that which is lost is of great worth to Him and must be found and *placed in*; or *restored to*; its rightful place.

In Luke 15:7b concerning the lost sheep its says, *"Rejoice with me, for I have found My sheep which was lost!"* and in Luke 15:9b concerning the lost coin its says, *"Rejoice with me, for I have found the piece (coin) which I lost!"*

Let us now move forward in this passage of scripture; and take a look at what most of us know as, *the parable of the prodigal son*. I like to call this the parable of.. *'A Father and two sons'.*
Many only look closely at the son that left the house as the prodigal. A closer look will show there is more to this part of the story, than we normally consider!

Luke 15:11-32 *"¹¹Then he said; "A certain man had two sons."* There was a father that had two sons. They were part of the same family, but so incredibly different! Not only were they sons of the same father, but they were also brothers. One older, one younger, different ages, different personalities, different likes and dislikes.

Just like two of Jesus closest disciples, James and John. The sons of thunder (Mark 3:17). This is where one of the great challenges of parenting lies, whether natural or spiritual.

Verse 12 tells us the younger son came looking for his inheritance. Sons have an inheritance and the younger son knew it. He wasn't afraid to ask for it and he knew his father really could not refuse him. The younger son wanted his inheritance right there and then, Why? Maybe he thought he would miss out, or it wouldn't be there for him if he waited till he was older. Maybe he thought his older brother would take everything before him and leave nothing!

The younger son thought he was ready to move on. He thought he was ready to possess all that was his. He was soon to discover he really wasn't ready at all! He never fully comprehended that his father worked hard, paid a high price and sacrificed much for both his sons to have an inheritance. This principal of sacrifice applies to spiritual fathers and mothers with their spiritual sons and daughters.

The younger son was like a child that is given a double barrel shot-gun that has great power and can do a lot of damage. He doesn't know what do to with it, but he knows how to pull the trigger. He is not yet properly trained to use it or to be a wise steward of it. Verse 13 says the younger son gathered all together and journeyed to a far country. This is typical of a person just wanting to do their our own thing or should I say, what they believe they should be doing.

The person just wants to get as far away as they possibly can, from that which is familiar. Away from those who know them so well, especially their father. Like the younger son, such a person is blinded to the point of not being able to see their own, full potential, that is yet to be unlocked. Like the younger son, such a person wants to get as far away as possible from boundaries, accountability and restraint. But of course God our Heavenly Father sees all that is happening in the persons life. The apostolic prophetic heart is given by God to the spiritual parent. The spiritual parent has the capacity to see and recognise the potential in the son or daughter that is being raised. That same apostolic prophetic heart brings restoration and encourages maturity in the one who has struggled with the results of being a prodigal.

When he got far away from his father's house, he wasted his possessions with prodigal living. Prodigal living is equal to being reckless and living loose. There is no restraint or self control. It is a path of self-destruction.

Proverbs 29:18 tells us *"Where there is no revelation, the people cast off restraint. But happy is he who keeps the law."*

Sons and daughters receive revelation from their fathers and mothers which brings restraint, self control and character development. Such revelation from a father or mother brings focus, and deals with aimless wandering and distractions. There is nothing like vision to deal with distraction that would otherwise lead to destruction. A Son must learn the principles that his father lives by; to be able to understand his father and live as his father lives. A son must learn for the sake of his longevity and lasting fruitfulness, if he is to build on what he gets from his father, whether natural or spiritual.

The younger son was the epitome of one who is called to be a son or daughter of God and ends up living like a *pauper,* that is:-one who has nothing, possesses nothing, no inheritance or a *vagabond* that is:- one who wanders or roams about, from place to place, having no fixed abode, no home!

Ultimately the prodigal is one who is called to be a son or daughter of God and ends up living like an *orphan,* that is one who has no parent! Whether in the house or outside the house, it makes no difference to the status of being a prodigal if the heart hasn't shifted or changed!

Jesus say's in John 14:18 *"I will not leave you orphans, I will come to you."* Thank God for His Holy Spirit who works in and through the spiritual parent, whilst working in the prodigal; to produce a son or daughter! He is the Spirit of adoption!

Romans 8:15 says
*"For you did not receive the **spirit of** bondage again to fear, but you received the **Spirit of adoption** by whom we cry out, "Abba, Father.""*

The Holy Spirit, through the apostolic prophetic heart, brings restoration to the sons and daughters of God. He is the one who will eventually reveal them all to the world.

There are many outside *the house* that is, *the family of God* that have wasted what the father has given them. This is where much of the resources of the kingdom of God have been tied up.

A principle truth to consider: Some of God's sons and daughters will only mature outside the house, that is outside the church setting as we know it. These are the ones that sometimes have found themselves *in the cave*, hidden, obscure out of man's sight, being *prepared* by the Father.

If we consider the life of David before he took the throne as King, he found himself in a cave along with his family and his four hundred men. Those who were discontented, discouraged, in debt etc., joined David in the cave of Adullam (1 Samuel 22:1-3) away from the schemes of King Saul. In David's case, his life needed to be spared and protected. Having to wait and be prepared for the appointed time, are among a number valid reasons why God the father will have His sons step outside *the house*.

David's *cave* experience could be compared to the *pig pen* experience of the younger son. Both experiences made way for God to do something in the individual, by way of testing or trial. Such experiences also make way for God to deal with the hearts of those who are as enemies, or opposed to the one whom God is preparing.

The Spirit of God is the one who brings them back in His appointed time. In the interim, the Father prepares the hearts of the fathers and mothers that will guide them into sonship when they return.

True fathers will expectantly wait, watch and pray for the return of the prodigal sons and daughters. They will be ready to train them and equip them, to fulfill their God given purpose.

True fathers and mothers are long suffering and wise......

*They know the heart

*They know their purpose

*They know their destiny and direction

*They know their weaknesses

*They know what it will take for the son or daughter to mature

*They know that it is grace, mercy and forgiveness that will hasten their development and return.

*They await the opportunity to train the son or daughter in righteousness (Hebrews 5: 14, Hebrews 12: 11)

True fathers remember it's the goodness of God, that leads a son or daughter to repentance.

Romans 2:4 *"Or do you despise the riches of His goodness, forbearance, and long-suffering, not knowing that the goodness of God leads you to repentance?"*

Fathers know that the sons and daughters of God have a rightful inheritance to possess and walk in.

He knows in turn they will have arrived, when they themselves become a true father or mother, or learn to think like a father or mother.

In verse 22 we see a true father's *response* is to bring out the best robe, a ring and sandals. He knows what the son is ready for!

1. The Best Robe = A Robe of Righteousness. A Mantle of Anointing. A physical sign of favour. A sign of love and grace, Just like Joseph and his coat of many colours, that was given to him by his father Jacob (Genesis 37:3-36).

2. Ring = A Seal of Authority. A sign of the higher authority that we are representative of as ambassadors. A son that carries the full endorsement of his father. Able to act on his behalf.

3. Sandals = Putting the shoes on our feet. A readiness to go and do business in the wider world. Akin to the *shoes of peace* spoken of in Ephesians 6:15. A readiness to go and preach the good news. To go and reap the harvest and make disciples.

According to the custom of the day, the son that had been given all three items, was a son that had the full power and authority of his father and his fathers household. He could act, transact and make decisions on behalf of the whole family.

Sometimes the younger son is misunderstood, because He is eager to embrace the father's vision and responsibility, not knowing what it costs. Just like Joseph with the dreams he had (Genesis 37:5-10). The favoured son's desire for the fulfilment, and to have the full power and authority that goes with it, provokes many thoughts and feelings in others. But he lacks the wisdom and foresight. He lacks the experience, but still:

1. He just wants to *have a go*.

2. He wants to grow and be considered mature and *grown up*. *He just isn't there yet*.

Sometimes eagerness to *have a go* is mistaken for rebellion or wrong motivation. But he is still a son, no matter what the circumstances. He just hasn't learned yet; to think and act as a son.

He doesn't yet know and understand the responsibility and liberty he has as a son. But it is his, by birth-right.

The scripture tells us in Proverbs 19:2 that it is dangerous to have zeal without knowledge. It also tells us that one who acts in haste makes poor choices. We also learn that, the bondage of *corruption* exists in all our lives until we are liberated from it!

Romans 8:21 tells us, *"because the creation itself also will be delivered from the bondage of corruption into the **glorious liberty of the children of God.**"*

Romans 11:28 has a principle in it, for us to understand. *"Concerning the gospel they are enemies for your sake, but concerning the election they are beloved for the sake of the fathers."* The apostle Paul wrote this scripture in relation to Israel's rejection of Christ as messiah, which has lead to an opportunity for Gentiles to accept Christ as messiah. The point is that those *outside* the house, *outside* the family, are just as *important* as those *inside* the house, *inside* the family. Those *outside* like Israel, can still come *in,* and become part of the family, just like the prodigal son!

As a spiritual father and an apostle, Paul demonstrates the apostolic prophetic heart of the Father perfectly, in his epistle to the Romans.

Verse 14 tells us that, the younger son had spent all and a famine arose. He began to be in want and he was now a long way from home. He now had to find his way home.

God the father is helping the sons and daughters to find their way home just like He did the prodigal son outside the house. We must be careful not to hinder them. It's easy for those of us in the house to *discourage* or *crush* those outside trying to *return* or find *a way* in. Just as the older son didn't understand the younger son, so too do those in the house today, not understand those outside the house.

Verse 15 tells us the younger son went and *joined* himself to a citizen of that country. In the Amplified version, that word *Joined* actually means, he *forced himself upon* or sought to be *glued to* a citizen of that country.

What was happening? He was looking to belong. He was alienated, Isolated and without the covering that a loving father provides. He had come to the end of himself. He was eating pig food. His resources had run out. He had spent and used up all of his inheritance. How many of us know that when your resources run out it's always a famine? He hadn't yet understood that his father had sown and reaped for him to have an inheritance. He hadn't yet learned to do the same as his father, that is, to sow and reap!

He was now trying to find his place. He was now trying to be a son in the *wrong* place. His sonship wasn't valid or accepted in the strange land. He needed a father a *true* father. *His* father. The father God had *given* him. The father that God had *chosen* for him.

In verse 17, we can see that the younger son got a revelation of the fathers house and the fathers love. He came to a realization of the father's care, protection and covering. After he came to his senses in the pig pen, he realized there was an abundance of food in his father's house and enough to spare.

Something to consider: If you are in *famine*, maybe you are in the *wrong place*?

Verse 18 *Younger son had to:*

1. *Acknowledge* the hindrance and blockage in his life.

2. Be *Humbled*

3. Become *Repentant*

Verse 19 *He got up & went to his father:*

1. He had to *Remove* himself from where he was to be where his sonship was *valid*.

2. His *sonship* was his *passport* to home and to his father.

3. He had to do something. He had to make a *move towards* his father,

He had to get up close and personal, and establish a new found *intimacy* with his father. This of course was all necessary for his restoration.

Now let's take a look at the older Son. The older son was the prodigal that never left the house! He lived as a servant in his fathers house. He fulfilled his part in a dutiful manner. He had no joy and no sense of understanding concerning his father's heart. He had access to everything that his younger brother had access to but had no relevant revelation or understanding of his inheritance. He was bitter v30, he was angry v28 and didn't realize or appreciate that he had a portion, that his father had prepared for him, already v32.

Because the older son (brother) had lived as a *servant* instead of as a *son* in his father's house Verse 29, he was miserable & nasty towards his younger brother (the younger son). Comparing, attacking, envious. So many have lived in Father God's house (the Church) in our present day; just like the older son. He treated his younger brother as an enemy because he didn't have the close connection and understanding with his father. Rivalry and competition are things that the fathers and mothers must deal with through the apostolic prophetic heart of God which is seen in restoration.

Relationship must precede anything else that we do in the *Father's house*. In John 15:15 Jesus said to his disciples *"No longer do I call you servants, for a servant does not know what his master is doing; but I have called you friends, for all things that I heard from My Father I have made known to you."*

Verse 25 "Now his older son was in the field"…….Always working, always busy. But never any joy. No time to laugh or smile.

Verse 26 He heard music and dancing. But he didn't know what it meant. He couldn't discern what was going on. He didn't understand what it meant to receive. To receive mercy and grace that liberates. Sons and daughters of God must understand the nature of receiving as well as giving!

The Father knew when to celebrate. He knew how to receive. The Father's ability to receive made way for restoration. The older son didn't understand this. He didn't know the fathers heart.

The sad truth is that the older son was serving *in the house,* but, didn't know the father's heart and so ending up living like he was outside the house, in the pig pen that his younger brother found himself in, in a foreign land.

He lived in the father's house but had no intimacy with the father. No relationship with the father. No love for his father, even though the father demonstrated it. There are many *in the house* like that today.

In verse 29 we see that the older son was bitter, critical, judgmental, feeling sorry for himself and stuck in self-pity. He looked only at what he thought he didn't have, rather than realizing what he had, and appreciating it.

For those of us who have been given the responsibility and the privilege of a spiritual parent, this is the one that we must pray for fervently, until he knows who he really is.

Sometimes the son that remains in the house is a bigger challenge than the one outside the house. Unless the son in the house has a *change of heart*, he will continue to *hinder* the growth of the family.

The older son didn't understand the celebration that was taking place. He didn't understand the purpose of Celebration. Our Heavenly Father's Heart, as well as the earthly father to these two sons, can be seen in verse 32 *"It was right that we should make merry and be glad, for your brother was dead and is alive again, and was lost and is found"*

What was dead has been made alive again and what was lost has been found. What a beautiful picture of the Father's heart this is. A beautiful picture of restoration. This is the apostolic prophetic heart that Father God is giving to His spiritual fathers and mothers, His holy apostles and prophets.

The father understood the purpose of Celebration. It was to help the process of restoration of the family member. It made the family part of the restoration process. It also helped the restored individual find their place of acceptance in the family. It helped them fit in and belong.

Celebration caused the older son to see the condition of his own heart/his own attitude. Celebration also caused the older son and younger son to see the father's heart, which neither of them had really understood.

Both the younger and older son needed to see what a true father's heart was really like. Celebration is part of a true father's heart. Celebration is part of the restoration heart of Father God.

Fathers will teach their sons to celebrate their victories in the right way. A victory for the individual family member is a victory for the whole family. All God's sons and daughters need to be able to celebrate with a son or daughter who gets a victory and experiences restoration. The word of God tells us in Romans 12:15, we are to *"Rejoice with those who rejoice, and weep with those who weep."*

The older son could have rejoiced with his father. But he was more concerned about what he thought he was missing out on; in terms of his inheritance. He was concerned that the younger son was squandering *his inheritance* as well. The older son was more concerned about the material things, than he was about having a good relationship with his brother and father. He couldn't rejoice and be happy with his younger brother and father.

God the Father wants his fathers and mothers, that is His apostles and prophets released and functioning, to bring forth the sons and daughters of God. This is where His restoration will take place. This is fatherhood and sonship, the divine pattern in motion.

It's time to place the robe of righteousness, that is a mantle of anointing on the sons and daughters of God. It's Time to put the ring on their finger as a seal of authority and help them exercise it. It's time to put the sandals on their feet, in readiness to go and preach the good news and reap a great harvest and make disciples that become true sons and daughters.

A bringing to maturity in character and Christ-likeness. An equipping in knowledge and skills. An anointing and gifting in the Spirit. All are necessary for the sons and daughters of God to arise and be revealed.

All things are being restored... Acts 3:21 *"whom heaven must receive until the times of restoration of all things, which God has spoken by the mouth of all His holy prophets since the world began"*

Many sons and daughters are being brought to glory....Hebrews 2:10 *"For it was fitting for Him, for whom are all things and by whom are all things, in bringing many sons to glory, to make the captain of their salvation perfect through sufferings."*

The revealing of the sons of God is still to happen. Romans 8: 19 *"For the earnest expectation of the creation eagerly waits for the revealing of the sons of God"*

Let us pray for the the sons and daughters in the house, as well as the sons and daughters outside of the house! Pray for their growth and maturity. Pray that they would know their identity in Him!

We are waiting with great expectation, along with all of creation, for the big unveiling ceremony. The heaven inspired and ordained graduation day.

The curtains on the stage that pass between heaven and earth, shall be rolled back and all shall see. What rejoicing and celebration there will be.

Let us pray that God creates many spiritual fathers and mothers, within the hearts of the apostles and prophets, that He will make to be instrumental in raising many sons and daughters of God. Amen!

***

2 Timothy 4:9-13

*"Be diligent to come to me quickly; ¹⁰for Demas has forsaken me, having loved this present world, and has departed for Thessalonica—Crescens for Galatia, Titus for Dalmatia. ¹¹****Only Luke is with me. Get Mark and bring him with you, for he is useful to me for ministry.*** *¹²And Tychicus I have sent to Ephesus. ¹³Bring the cloak that I left with Carpus at Troas when you come—and the books, especially the parchments."*

***

CHAPTER FOUR

Becoming a Father!

Becoming a Father and Passing the Baton

Abraham was 75 years of age when he was first promised a son by God (Genesis 12:1-3) At the age of 100 years, which was 25 years later, he received the fulfillment of the promised son, Isaac (Genesis 21:5). This became the period of time that Jehovah God used to test and shape Abraham's character. In this time period the promise became a covenant between God and Abraham (Genesis 15:1-17). This was a necessary part of the process, for him to be made ready to be the father he needed to be, to receive and produce his promised son Isaac.

By definition we can say that a father is technically not a father in reality, until he has a son, but God changed Abram's name to Abraham (Genesis 17:1-8) in anticipation, reassurance and as a reminder of what was to come! The name change also represented a change of heart and thinking in readiness for the promised son to be received. Calling things that be not as though they are, was God's heart and mind towards Abraham.

Romans 4:16-18 "*¹⁶Therefore it is of faith that it might be according to grace, so that the promise might be sure to all the seed, not only to those who are of the law, but also to those who are of the faith of Abraham,* *who is the father of us all* [17] *(as it is written, "I have made you a father of many nations") in the presence of Him whom he believed—God, who gives life to the dead and calls those things which do not exist as though they did;* [18] *who, contrary to hope, in hope believed, so that he became the father of many nations, according to what was spoken, "So shall your descendants be."*

God knew that Abraham was desperate to have an heir to pass on what He had been given. Genesis 15:1 *"And Abram said, "You have given me no children; so a servant in my household will be my heir." Then the word of the LORD came to him: "This man will not be your heir, but a son coming from your own body will be your heir."*

Isaac would eventually become the heir, the receiver of the baton of promise and covenant. It would pass to him, so that eventually he could pass it on to the son that he would have in Jacob.

We see the passing of the baton of covenant (2 Samuel 7), along with inheritance and the throne in the life of Solomon even after the death of his father King David:

1 Kings 8:22-26 *"*[25]*Therefore, Lord God of Israel, now keep what You promised Your servant David my father, saying, 'You shall not fail to have a man sit before Me on the throne of Israel, only if your sons take heed to their way, that they walk before Me as you have walked before Me."*

Solomon was a son to David according God's natural order, but had spiritually based covenants and prophetic promises attached to his sonship.

Yet again as follows, a different kind of example with Elijah and Elisha. Elisha was as a son to Elijah according to God's spiritual order. But in the natural order he was Shaphat's son (1 Kings 19:16,19, 2 kings 3:11). Elisha's connection to Elijah as a son, was one of the heart and the Spirit. This highlights a true spiritual father and son relationship.

2 Kings 2:14-15a *"¹⁴Then he took the mantle of Elijah that had fallen from him, and struck the water, and said, "Where is the Lord God of Elijah?" And when he also had struck the water, it was divided this way and that; and Elisha crossed over. ¹⁵Now when the sons of the prophets who were from Jericho saw him, they said, "The spirit of Elijah rests on Elisha."*

Apostle Paul's life is another example of a spiritual father in the making. From the time of his conversion when he met the risen Lord Jesus Christ on the road to Damascus (Acts 9:3-7), to the time of his latter ministry some 10 or more years later, we see that he had matured greatly.

The scripture tells us in Acts 9:17-19 that as soon as Paul received his sight through the laying on of Ananias hands, he arose and was baptised. He then ate and was strengthened. He spent time with the disciples, then Verse 20 tells us *"immediately he preached the Christ in the synagogues, that He is the son of God,"* He confounded many. Many believed. There were those who questioned and said isn't this the one who persecuted and killed many of the Christians? Many of the Jews plotted and wanted to kill him! The disciples found out and eventually sent him away to Caesarea and then on to Tarsus. They had to protect his life(Acts 9:23-30). One could say that Paul had to be tempered by God for a season. He was strong, fiery, passionate, impatient and God had to protect him and the Church.

Straight after Paul was taken off the scene we read the following in Acts 9:31. *"³¹Then the churches throughout all Judea, Galilee, and Samaria had peace and were edified. And walking in the fear of the Lord and in the comfort of the Holy Spirit, they were multiplied."*

God had to do His work in Paul to make him not only the apostle but also the spiritual father the Church of Jesus Christ would need in time, along with the many sons and daughters that would be raised through him, in the Christian faith.

As an apostle he gained great wisdom, knowledge, perseverance and understanding. His level of revelation (2 Corinthians 12:1-10) was commensurate with how much he suffered, as he grew in the apostolic prophetic heart. Paul went from being the impatient, strong-willed, hard headed, zealous law keeper and enforcer to the loving, patient, firm but gentle spiritual father, and sometimes authoritative apostle of Jesus Christ (Philippians 3:4-11). The result was that Paul was able to produce sons and daughters!

A Father's character flaws and weaknesses need to be dealt with and his strengths refined, for him to become the father God needs him to be. The testing of his faith is necessary to learn to work in partnership with the Spirit of God and for him to facilitate reproducing Christ-like qualities in the sons and daughters of God. In fact, in reality, a father must first learn what it means to be a son, if he is to be a father with the apostolic prophetic heart of God.

A father draws from his own experience as a son, which equips him to know how to guide, develop and bring correction to a son in the faith with a heart of love and grace. The apostolic prophetic heart of God in the apostle and prophet encourages a son to be a partaker of the divine nature (2 Peter 1: 3-4).

Examples of fathers and sons:

*Father Abraham and Isaac (Genesis 22:2)

*Elijah, Elisha and the sons of the prophets (1 Kings 19:19,21, 2 Kings 2:1-9, 2 Kings 2:15)

*Apostle Paul and Timothy (1 Corinthians 4:17, 1 Tim. 1:2,18, 2 Tim. 1:2)

*King David and Solomon (1 Kings 2:1, Nehemiah 12:45)

*God the Father and Jesus (John 3:16, 2 Corinthians 1:19)

*Jesus and the 12 disciples. (John 14:7,9)

Abraham's name was changed from *Abram* to *Abraham*. Abram meaning *father of a nation* to Abraham meaning *father of many nations*.(Genesis 17:1-8) God wants many sons and daughters brought to Glory!

Hebrews 2:10 *"For it was fitting for Him, for whom are all things and by whom are all things, in bringing many sons to glory, to make the captain of their salvation perfect through sufferings."*

Jesus suffering was with an eternal purpose in mind; given to Him by His Father. The redemptive work at Calvary was to produce after Himself, not just one son or daughter, but rather many sons and daughters.

As apostle Paul said in Galatians 4:19b concerning his spiritual children *"of whom I travail in birth again until Christ be formed in you"*. The spiritual father or mother labours and travails to see the maturity and growth of their sons and daughters. They ultimately watch and pray, waiting to see Christ formed within.

A good principle to understand and learn from Abraham's life is that, eventually we have to offer up our sons and daughters to Father God. The apostolic prophetic heart of God in the apostle and prophet ultimately recognises that the sons and daughters belong to God, and He will ultimately do with them what he wants. This is the way we will see many sons and daughters reproduced and brought to Glory. Just as God our Father did with Jesus, and Abraham did with Isaac, offering our sons and daughters up to God means that we are letting God determine their potential, their boundaries and their destiny.

The apostolic prophetic heart of God in the mature apostle and prophet trusts God as Heavenly Father and releases the individual, rather than trying to control and manipulate the outcomes and destiny of the individual. True fathers know their sons and daughters and true sons and daughters know their fathers.

In Genesis 22:1-18 Abraham offers Isaac up to God. In Genesis 21:11-14 Abraham sends Hagar and her son Ishmael away to make room for the promise and purpose of God to be fulfilled through Isaac's life. We often need to wait for God to show us who our sons are to be. Sometimes to father a true son we must make room by dealing with impatience and all the associated obstacles. Abraham thought he could make it happen by going along with his wife Sarah's plan, to have a child by her maid servant Hagar.

True sons are needed to impart to, from the Spirit and the anointing, and to pass on an inheritance. In Abraham's case his destiny and purpose in God was to be perpetual, from generation to generation, through his promised son Isaac and grandson Jacob and to continue on down the line through Judah until we get to Christ the Son of God.

As long as there is a true son to partake of the divine nature and walk in Godly ways, there will always be opportunity for the apostolic prophetic heart of God to pass on the baton of inheritance, blessing, promise and anointing through His holy apostles and prophets.

A good word for fathers to live by, to role model, and to teach their sons and daughters can be found in James 4:10 *"Humble yourselves in the sight of the Lord, and He will lift you up."* also in
2 Chronicles 7:14 it says *"if My people who are called by My name will humble themselves, and pray and seek My face, and turn from their wicked ways, then I will hear from heaven, and will forgive their sin and heal their land."*

Deuteronomy 30:19-20 [19b] *"....therefore choose life, that both you and your descendants may live."* Both fathers and mothers, and sons and daughters are a key to future generations.

Fathers are made through a process and the workings of the Holy Spirit. They are not born fathers. One may be a father because of the birth of a son or daughter, but the relationship dynamics & lessons learned to function as father come through a process of growth and change.

It is the same with sons and daughters. They are made through a process, not born! The relationship, heart and function need to catch up to the title and birthright of a son or daughter.

Fathers have an inbuilt quality given by God that is supercharged by the Holy Spirit. When they walk with God as spiritual fathers and as followers of Christ, the apostolic prophetic heart of God is stirred.

It enables them to make sacrifice, empower, equip, validate, train, discipline, correct, set boundaries, pass on knowledge and most importantly to help establish a healthy identity in the son or daughter of God.

Let us pray that mature, travailing, interceding spiritual fathers and mothers will be raised and brought forth with the apostolic prophetic heart of God. That they will have grace and strength given by God to stand with, and see the sons and daughters of God brought forth in the earth! Amen!

***

Malachi 4:6
*"And he will turn **the hearts of the fathers to the children**, And **the hearts of the children to their fathers**, Lest I come and strike the earth with a curse."*

***

CHAPTER FIVE

The Revealing of the Sons of God!

Romans 8:19 says *"For the earnest expectation of the creation eagerly waits for the revealing of the Sons of God."*

I believe one of the biggest parts of the apostolic prophetic heart of God is the restoration and the revealing of His sons and daughters.

Malachi 4:6 tells us, He will turn the hearts of the fathers to the children and the hearts of the children to the fathers. It is both a truth and a principle that must happen according to the natural and spiritual order of things that God has created.

God is giving His father heart to those He gives the mantle of apostle and prophet. These are the spiritual fathers and mothers with great maturity and Christ-likeness that God will use, to bring forth His sons and daughters firstly into the spirit realm and secondly into the earth, where they will be made manifest.

God our Heavenly Father wants Sons

Many of God's sons are living with a *servant, slave* mentality. Unable to see what they have been offered. Unable to possess what the Father has promised. It is the spiritual fathers and mothers that will confront the servant, slave mentality, revealing a true son or daughter. It is only the *true spiritual sons and daughters* that have the *mentality and heart of a son*, that will reveal His Glory.

His *sons and daughters* will be a part of the prime mover He uses, to bring about the restoration of all things to Himself. The restoration of all things will continue to be activated and enabled by the apostolic prophetic heart that He is gives to His apostles and prophets. The apostolic prophetic heart of God in His ministers, will enable them to be true spiritual parents producing true and mature, spiritual sons and daughters.

If there are no fathers and mothers, there can be no revealed sons and daughters. But equally true is the fact that, if we produce no sons and daughters then there will be no future fathers and mothers in the faith.

True spiritual fathers bring the heart of the Father (God in heaven) to bear upon the next generation to produce sons. Fathers are needed to prepare the way for God's generational blessings to be passed on. If there are no fathers, there can be no passing on of the blessings.

Passing on of God the Father's blessings, gifts and responsibilities can be equated to, and illustrated by the passing of a baton. The divine pattern of fatherhood and sonship requires that we have someone to pass and someone to receive the Baton.

Many churches, ministries, revivals, gifts and callings have failed to move from generation to generation due to a failure to understand that the baton must be passed from generation to generation. From fathers and mothers to sons and daughters.

In time past, much of what was referred to as a *generation gap*, was the result of a breakdown of relationship and therefore a break down of communication leading to a lack of understanding.

We can not and we must not drop the baton. A father's responsibility is to pass on the charge of his Heavenly Father to his sons. We see it in the life of Paul with Timothy, and we see it in the life of King David with Solomon.

1 Timothy 1:18 *"This **charge** I commit to you, son Timothy, according to the prophecies previously made concerning you, that by them you may wage the good warfare."*

The charge given to Timothy involved a prophetic impartation! Timothy was to wage a good warfare according to those prophecies and the associated gifts imparted to him, through the laying on of an apostolic spiritual father's hands.

Batons can be passed apostolically and prophetically from a father to a son. As with Paul and Timothy, we see this in the life of Elijah and Elisha. When Elijah was taken by chariots of fire (2 Kings 2:12), Elisha had to be there. The anointing that Elijah carried in his ministry as a prophet, needed to be passed to one who had been as a son to him (2 Kings 2:13-14).

We see it in the life of King David and his son Solomon in

1 Kings 2:1-4 *"Now the days of David drew near that he should die, and he **charged** Solomon his son, saying: ²"I go the way of all the earth; be strong, therefore, and prove yourself a man. ³And keep the charge of the Lord your God: to walk in His ways, to keep His statutes, His commandments, His judgments, and His testimonies, as it is written in the Law of Moses, that you may prosper in all that you do and wherever you turn; ⁴that the Lord may fulfill His word which He spoke concerning me, saying, 'If your sons take heed to their way, to walk before Me in truth*

with all their heart and with all their soul,' He said, 'you shall not lack a man on the throne of Israel.'

David was anointed as a king and needed to be able to pass the baton of his kingship responsibility, to one who had the birthright of an heir. Of course Solomon as a son had the birthright to be able to receive the baton that carried great responsibility.

The passing of the baton and everything it represents, contributes to the revealing of a son or daughter! The anointing upon a king is akin to the anointing upon an apostle, and so the apostolic prophetic heart of God carries the charge given to a son or daughter in the faith. This makes manifest what is in the heart of the one receiving the baton.

We know of course from a previous chapter in the book, entitled "A Father and Two Sons" that the possessing of the prodigal son's inheritance ahead of time, proved what was in his heart. It proved initially that he was an immature son. It led him to a pig pen and a humbled position, away from his father in a foreign land. But it proved to be his making, rather than his total destruction! Because of the right response of his heart, and the eventual repentant attitude of his mind, he found his way back.

Fatherlessness

Fatherlessness is the scourge of our times. It brings with it dysfunctionality and a loss of healthy family connection. A spiritual father's identity helps build the son or daughter's identity enabling them to receive the baton. This is in part where the *revealing* of the sons and daughters will take place.

No Father and no mother means, orphaned children. Father God doesn't want to see sons and daughters orphaned, neither does he want to see orphaned spiritual families or churches.

Fatherlessness means a loss of connection and a lack of role-modelling. It means no anchor, no direction, no purpose, because of a lack of mentoring that would normally come with a father or mother.

A healthy balanced family has a father, mother and sons and daughters, both in the natural and the spiritual.

In a family one can see that there are babes, young children, teenagers and young adults along with the parents. In the spiritual sense as God's people, we are all His children, but we are not all on the same level of spiritual maturity and *we are not all necessarily* a son or daughter in heart or mind.

The apostle John highlights this truth for us, by the way he addresses the believers in his epistle.

> In 1 John 2:12-14 he writes:

*¹² "I write to you **little children**,*
  Because your sins are forgiven you for His name's sake.
*¹³ "I write to you, **fathers**,*
  Because you have known Him who is from the beginning.
  *I write to you, **young men**,*
  Because you have overcome the wicked one.
  *I write to you, **little children**,*
  *Because you have known the **Father**."*
*¹⁴ "I have written to you, **fathers**,*
  Because you have known Him who is from the beginning.
  *I have written to you, **young men**,*
  Because you are strong, and the word of God abides in you,
  And you have overcome the wicked one."

Hebrews 5:12 tells us that spiritual babes partake of milk and are unskilled in the word of righteousness.

Hebrews 5:14 tells us that solid food is for those of full age, who by reason of use have their senses exercised to discern good and evil.

Sons and daughters should aim to eventually become fathers & mothers spiritually, just as the disciple should aim to become one who makes disciples.

Hebrews 5:12a *For though by this time you ought to be teachers..."*

We are to graduate from student to becoming the teacher, the mentor, the enabler. *"This we will do if God permits"* as the writer of Hebrews says in chapter 6 and verse 3.

Fathers & Mothers mean family, and family means:

- A vital connection.
- A sense of security, love and intimacy.
- A sense of identity.
- A sense of belonging and fitting in.
- A place to serve.
- A sense of knowing ones place.

Family is first *relational* and second *organisational*. Hence the need for the apostolic and prophetic heart that mature apostles and prophets bring. In fact family is to be an *organism* rather than an *organisation*. This applies in both the natural family as well as the spiritual family.

Structure and Order in God's family is to be derived from the spiritual and relational maturity of its members. Hence the fathers and mothers, and sons and daughters.

John chapter 15 paints for us a great picture of relationship among believers in God's family, in terms of us being compared to a *vine* and its *branches*. Jesus being the *true vine*, and the children i.e. the *sons and daughters* of God, being *the branches*. Then it says that Father God is the *vine dresser* who prunes the branches.

A truth to consider: You may be the only connection that an individual has with His family, the church. The vine and the branches illustrate this point in the gospel of John 15:1-15. Every branch is connected to the vine but not every branch is connected directly to one another.

John 15:1-5 *"I am the true vine, and My Father is the vinedresser. ²Every branch in Me that does not bear fruit He takes away; and every branch that bears fruit He prunes, that it may bear more fruit. ³You are already clean because of the word which I have spoken to you.⁴Abide in Me, and I in you. As the branch cannot bear fruit of itself, unless it abides in the vine, neither can you, unless you abide in Me. ⁵"I am the vine, you are the branches. He who abides in Me, and I in him, bears much fruit; for without Me you can do nothing."*

God gave His Son (singular) to produce sons (plural), that He might connect them to the *true vine*, that is *His family*.

Let us also not forget, that through the whole process, the Father's redemptive purpose is front and centre according to the divine pattern of fatherhood and sonship.

The Holy Spirit, the Spirit of a*doption*, hastens towards the raising, restoring and revealing of the sons and daughters of God. The apostolic prophetic heart of God in the apostle and prophet looks for, wrestles for, the revealing of a son or daughter, born of the Spirit of God.

****
Ephesians 1:3-6

"³Blessed be the God and Father of our Lord Jesus Christ, who has blessed us with every spiritual blessing in the heavenly places in Christ, ⁴just as He chose us in Him before the foundation of the world, that we should be holy and without blame before Him in love, ⁵having predestined us to adoption as sons by Jesus Christ to Himself, according to the good pleasure of His will, ⁶to the praise of the glory of His grace, by which He made us accepted in the Beloved."
****

CHAPTER SIX

Character Qualities found in a Spiritual Son or Daughter!

Reproducing and Revealing Character Qualities!

Much of what the New Testament has to say to us about the practicalities of the divine pattern of fatherhood and sonship, is seen in apostle Paul's relationship with Timothy.

Paul and Timothy's relationship spans an approximate 20 year period judging by the writing of the epistles. There are others also, that Paul relates to as a spiritual father, such as the Corinthians and the Galatians.

Predominantly we learn from the practical details and spiritual principles, shared in Paul and Timothy's relationship, found mostly in 1 Timothy and 2 Timothy which highlights the revealed qualities of a true spiritual son or daughter.

It is in Acts chapter 16 verses 1-5 on Paul's second missionary journey, that we first pick up on the beginning of the relationship between Paul and Timothy.

"⁵Then he came to Derbe and Lystra. And behold, a certain disciple was there, named Timothy, the son of a certain Jewish woman who believed, but his father was Greek. ²He was well spoken of by the brethren who were at Lystra and Iconium. ³Paul wanted to have him go on with him. And he took him and circumcised him because of the Jews who were in that region, for they all knew that his father was Greek. ⁴And as they went through the cities, they delivered to them the decrees to keep, which were determined by the apostles and elders at Jerusalem. ⁵So the churches were strengthened in the faith, and increased in number daily."

Paul became a spiritual father to Timothy, teaching him and demonstrating to him the principles and truths of the Christian faith and ministry. This brought him to maturity in character and fruitfulness in Christian service.

The Following is a list of character qualities, that were taught and modelled by Paul for Timothy his son; in the faith and ministry:

These are qualities that a true father or mother in the faith longs to see reproduced in a son or daughter of God.

Faithfulness - 2 Timothy 2:2 *"And the things that you have heard from me among many witnesses, commit these to faithful men who will be able to teach others also."* Faithful in *the little* always makes way for a good foundation for being faithful in *the much*.

Purity - (a clean vessel) 2 Timothy 2:20-22 *"²⁰But in a great house there are not only vessels of gold and silver, but also of wood and clay, some for honor and some for dishonor. ²¹Therefore if anyone cleanses himself from the latter, he will be a vessel for honor, sanctified and useful for the Master, prepared for every good work. ²²Flee also youthful lusts; but pursue righteousness, faith, love, peace with those who call on the Lord out of a pure heart."*

Honour - (the elder, father or mother in the faith) 1 Timothy 5:17 *"Let the elders who rule well be counted worthy of double honour, especially those who labor in the word and doctrine."*

Supportive of the Spiritual Father & his ministry - Philippians 2:19 *"But I trust in the Lord Jesus to send Timothy to you shortly, that I also may be encouraged when I know your state"* The son or daughter in the faith learning the principle of serving the Spiritual Father or Mother, makes way for many lessons to be learned and for great impartation to take place. It is the *'caught rather than taught'* principle in action. It is where much is gained based on the idea of *apprenticeship* or *mentorship* in action.

Teachable - (he was reminded and instructed consistently, and he received it) 1 Timothy 4:16 *"Take heed to yourself and to the doctrine. Continue in them, for in doing this you will save both yourself and those who hear you."*

Accuracy & Integrity - (studies to show himself approved) 2 Timothy 2:15 *"Be diligent to present yourself approved to God, a worker who does not need to be ashamed, rightly dividing the word of truth."*

Faithful Steward - 1 Corinthians 4:2 *"Moreover it is required in stewards that one be found faithful."* A good steward in natural/material and spiritual things.

Endure Hardship - (like a soldier) 2 Timothy 2:3-4 *"You therefore must endure hardship as a good soldier of Jesus Christ. ⁴No one engaged in warfare entangles himself with the affairs of this life, that he may please him who enlisted him as a soldier."*

Obedient & Submissive - (to a father or mother in the faith) Hebrews 13:17 *"Obey those who rule over you, and be submissive, for they watch out* *for your souls, as those who must give account. Let them do so with joy and not with grief, for that would be unprofitable for you.*

Discipline - (of an athlete) 2 Timothy 2:5 *"And also if anyone competes in athletics, he is not crowned unless he competes according to the rules."*

Sacrifice & Self-Discipline - 1 Corinthians 9:24-26 *"Do you not know that those who run in a race all run, but one receives the prize? Run in such a way that you may obtain it. ²⁵And everyone who competes for the prize is temperate in all things. Now they do it to obtain a perishable crown, but we for an imperishable crown. ²⁶Therefore I run thus: not with uncertainty. Thus I fight: not as one who beats the air."*

Industrious/Hard working - (like the farmer) 2 Timothy 2:6 *"The hardworking farmer must be first to partake of the crops."*

Gentleness & Humility - (correcting those who have been deceived) 2 Timothy 2:23-26 *"But avoid foolish and ignorant disputes, knowing that they generate strife. ²⁴And a servant of the Lord must not quarrel but be gentle to all, able to teach, patient, ²⁵in humility correcting those who are in opposition, if God perhaps will grant them repentance, so that they may know the truth, ²⁶and that they may come to their senses and escape the snare of the devil, having been taken captive by him to do his will."*

Rick Warren, Senior Pastor of Saddleback Church teaches as per his article posted on pastors.com dated the 6th February 2014, what he calls *'The three phases of a Paul & Timothy Relationship'* as follows:

1. Parenthood - 1 Timothy 1:2 *"my true son in the faith"* this is where parenthood is highlighted.

2. Pace-Setting - 2 Timothy 3:10-11 This is Paul being an example. He becomes a pace setter for Timothy to emulate.

3. Partnering - Romans 16:21 is where Timothy is recognised as a colleague & ministry partner to Paul. More of an equal who has arrived in maturity, status and experience

Rick Warren's teaching highlights what the author of this book has already stated, that is: *spiritual sons and daughters should aim to become spiritual fathers and mothers.*

Infancy to adulthood in the faith & ministry is what we see in Timothy's life under the spiritual fathering of the great and humble apostle Paul.

If a spiritual father or mother in the faith has learned to live and walk as a son then they have the capacity to reproduce the above listed qualities in the son or daughter, that will eventually lead those chosen, to become spiritual fathers and mothers, repeating the process!

As Paul tells Timothy in 1 Timothy 2:2 commit to faithful men that they may be able to teach others!

Philippians 2:20-22 "*²⁰For I have no one like-minded, who will sincerely care for your state. ²¹For all seek their own, not the things which are of Christ Jesus. ²²But you know his proven character, that as a son with his father he served with me in the gospel.*"

Paul's words here in this epistle to the Philippians, highlights the godly character reproduced in Timothy. It showed the love and sacrifice Timothy was prepared to make, in following Paul and serving Christ in the ministry.

Father to son, generation to generation! Fruit is produced and reproduced through this divine pattern of fatherhood and sonship.

This divine pattern shows that God uses a spiritual father or mother to shape the character of the son or daughter, whilst at the same time, God is shaping the son or daughter's destiny.

God the Father's order is always preparation before manifestation in everything, whether a son or daughter of God is being revealed, or a new ministry is being birthed and sent forth!

***

Philippians 2:19-21

"But I trust in the Lord Jesus to send Timothy to you shortly, that I also may be encouraged when I know your state. **²⁰For I have no one like-minded, who will sincerely care for your state.** *²¹For all seek their own, not the things which are of Christ Jesus."*

***

CHAPTER SEVEN

Restoring the Revelation!

Hebrews 1:1-4 *"God, who at various times and in various ways spoke in time past to the fathers by the prophets, ²has in these last days spoken to us by His Son, whom He has appointed heir of all things, through whom also He made the worlds; ³who being the brightness of His glory and the express image of His person, and upholding all things by the word of His power, when He had by Himself purged our sins, sat down at the right hand of the Majesty on high, ⁴having become so much better than the angels, as He has by inheritance obtained a more excellent name than they."*

God has been speaking *to* His creation, and *through* His creation since time began! When God speaks, there is always a revealing that takes place, if we have an ear to hear, as it says Revelation 2:7,11,17,29 Revelation 3:6,13,22. He has spoken through the prophets of old and through His revealed word. He has spoken to us through the purpose and the design found in everything that shows His finger-prints and bears His mark as the maker.

There is *revelation* and there is *revelation knowledge*. There is revelations and there is *revelations*. Then there is *the revelation* of *all* revelations. What am I talking about? I am talking about *the revelation of the person of Christ* to us all.

Once and for all through His Son, we have heard Him speak to us. The revelation comes to us personally through what He has done for us through His Son Jesus Christ, when our spirit is brought to life and the connection is established between us and God. Just like a snuffed out candle, that has been lit or re-lit, bringing with it light, that allows us to receive the revelation of Christ that the father has always wanted us to have!

John 1:4-5 *"⁴ In Him was life, and the life **was the light of men**. ⁵And the **light shines in the darkness**, and the darkness did not comprehend it."*

Proverbs 20:27 says *"The spirit of a man is the lamp of the Lord, searching all the inner depths of his heart."* The spirit of a man lit by the light of God, that is Christ with-in, is what brings the revelation that God wants a man or woman to receive!

Jesus Christ is the *revelation* of all revelations. He is the one who existed before He was born. Everything has been created by Him, through Him and for Him. Without Him, apart from Him, nothing exists.

Colossians 1:16 *"For by Him all things were created that are in heaven and that are on earth, visible and invisible, whether thrones or dominions or principalities or powers. All things were created through Him and for Him."*

He continues to bring that same message and revelation to us, through those He has chosen and appointed to represent Him. Especially through his apostles and prophets, his fathers and mothers to the family of God. Those who seek to produce sons and daughters for God must bear the mark of that revelation, which is seen in a transformed life.

The person of Jesus Christ, the resurrected, glorified Son of God, is the revelation that we all need, not just the crucified, bleeding, whipped and beaten Saviour. The Lion, not just the Lamb must be revealed.

Jesus must be revealed to the world. We must no longer hide Him from the Church or humanity! The gospel of Jesus Christ must be preached in all its fullness, uncompromisingly, and with power!

Jesus can and should be revealed in at least one of four ways to the individual person:

1. Through the *Word of God* (Bible)

2. By the *Holy Spirit* in dreams, visions and revelations!

3. The *Example* set by the spiritual fathers and mothers, especially the apostles and prophets!

4. Christ *Appearing* to the individual!

There are those in our day, that are receiving great revelations of the Lord Jesus Christ, just as the early disciples did shortly after His resurrection! There are many testimonies of people from other *faiths,* where Christ has appeared and spoken to the person, leading them to saving faith and delivering them from their dire circumstances.

Let us also consider Stephen the first Christian martyr's experience. At the time of his stoning and at the point of his death, he saw Jesus standing at the Father's right hand in glory!

Acts 7:55-56 *"But he, being full of the Holy Spirit, gazed into heaven and saw the glory of God, and Jesus standing at the right hand of God, ^{56}and said, "Look! I see the heavens opened and the Son of Man standing at the right hand of God!"*

When Jesus asked His disciples the question in Matthew 16:13, *"Who do men say that I, the Son of Man, am?"* He wasn't really seeking for peoples opinions about Himself. He was probing the disciples hearts, to see if they had gotten any heaven sent revelation from the Father about who He really is. The answer He received from the disciples was very *telling!* It gave Jesus the opportunity to encourage them and get a personal answer.

They had been with Him and he wanted to know if they got the revelation yet. Had His Father been able to reveal to them who He really is? Had they crossed over from the natural to the spiritual in their understanding? Were they seeing beyond what others were seeing externally?

In verse 14 they say to Him, *"some say John the Baptist, some Elijah, and others Jeremiah or one of the prophets"* Then Jesus makes the question a little more personal. In verse 15, He asks them, *"But who do you say that I am?"* In verse 16, Peter the spokesman for the group says, *"You are the Christ, the Son of the living God"*

Jesus affirms Peters revelation in verse 17, by stating that *"for flesh and blood has not revealed this to you, but My Father who is in heaven"* Jesus tells Peter that He is *blessed* for having received this revelation from His Heavenly Father!

The revelation that Peter received was life changing. It was the beginning of a change in his identity, purpose and destiny! Verse 18 says *"And I also say to you that you are Peter, and on this rock I will build My Church, and the gates of Hades shall not prevail against it"*

Peter's revelation of Jesus along with the other disciples, was the beginning of making way for His Church to be built on the right and proper foundations. Which is the revelation of Christ the Son of the living God. No other revelation, no other knowledge, no philosophy, no ideology, no other teaching will ever suffice.

Christ and Christ alone is the foundation, the cornerstone, the cap stone. He is the *stone* that the builders rejected. He is *the revelation* that makes the Church unstoppable and immovable! Apostle Paul states in

Ephesians 2:20 *"having been built on the foundation of the apostles and prophets, Jesus Christ Himself being the chief cornerstone,"*

The apostolic prophetic heart of God desires to know Christ and make Him known from a heart of sincerity and purity. Matthew 5:8 says *"Blessed are the pure in heart, for they shall see God."* and the pure in heart make Him known to those who need the revelation. The apostolic prophetic heart of God seeks to reproduce that in the sons and daughters of God.

Paul shares his heart with us in Philippians 3:10 when he says *"that I may know Him and the power of His resurrection, and the fellowship of His sufferings, being conformed to His death"*

Paul's whole life in Christ was born out of a powerful, Damascus road revelation experience, which led to him being blinded in his natural sight for three days, to allow for his spiritual eyes to be opened and for Him to see and know the risen Christ. Paul would need this *"heavenly vision"* to under gird his faith and ministry, and to constantly remind Him of Jesus and His sufferings as he engaged in answering the call, as an apostle and father in the faith to many sons and daughters!

Apostle John's revelation of Jesus Christ as recorded in Revelation chapter one, while on the Island of Patmos, was the direct result of his faithfulness and longevity in walking with Christ! He had persevered through many tests, trials and tribulations. Apostle John suffered much and offered great strength to the church through his example!

Revelation 1:12-18 *"[12] Then I turned to see the voice that spoke with me. And having turned I saw seven golden lampstands, [13] and in the midst of the seven lampstands One like the Son of Man, clothed with a garment down to the feet and girded about the chest with a golden band. [14] His head and hair were white like wool, as white as snow, and His eyes like a flame of fire; [15] His feet were like fine brass, as if refined in a furnace, and His voice as the sound of many waters; ¹⁶He had in His right hand seven stars, out of His mouth went a sharp two-edged sword, and His countenance was like the sun shining in its strength. ¹⁷And when I saw Him, I fell at His feet as dead. But He laid His right hand on me, saying to me, "Do not be afraid; I am the First and the Last. ¹⁸I am He who lives, and was dead, and behold, I am alive forevermore. Amen. And I have the keys of Hades and of Death."*

The apostolic prophetic heart of God in the apostle and prophet reveals Jesus; and therefore helps people to know the Father. Apostle Paul shows us this through his example, in the way he lived and what he taught.

Acts 20:18-21 "*¹⁸And when they had come to him, he said to them: "You know, from the first day that I came to Asia, in what manner I always lived among you, ¹⁹serving the Lord with all humility, with many tears and trials which happened to me by the plotting of the Jews; ²⁰***how I kept back nothing that was helpful, but proclaimed it to you***, and taught you publicly and from house to house, ²¹testifying to Jews, and also to Greeks, repentance toward God and faith toward our Lord Jesus Christ.*"

Acts 20:27 "*For I have not shunned, to declare to you the whole counsel of God.*" Apostle Paul's relationship to Jesus and the example he set, along with the doctrine he taught, was great preparation for revelation and manifestation of Christ in those he spiritually fathered!

The heart of God is seen in Jesus Christ, and Jesus Christ must be revealed to know the heart of God!

John 14:8 Phillip's question to Jesus concerning seeing the Father. "*Show us the Father and it is sufficient for us.*" Jesus answer to Phillip can be read in the next verse, "*⁹He who has seen Me has seen the Father*"

Thousands today, just like Phillip, are crying out *"show us the Father"*. Others say *"we want to see this Jesus you talk about."*

We know that our adversary the devil, has blinded the eyes of many people (2 Corinthians 4:4). But for the most part, we have kept Jesus hidden from people, by the religious things that we do!

Jesus asked the following question of His disciples once He was revealed.....

John 14:10 *"Do you not believe that I am in the Father, and the Father in Me? The words that I speak to you I do not speak on My own authority; but the Father who dwells in Me does the works."*

The modern day church has done so much that has actually hidden Jesus from both the regenerated (born again believer), and the unregenerate (unsaved) person

Jesus has been hidden from the everyday person by all the:

-Religious trappings, rituals, programs.

-Titles used by those in leadership.

-Rules, regulations, formulas and philosophies etc..

-Organisational structures.

-Lack of good role-modelling

In many places in these latter days, the church in general, has embraced a *form of godliness* and denied the inward transformational power that the apostolic prophetic heart of God brings through the apostle and prophet, in preaching the unadulterated gospel. The principle holds true. If they rejected Me they will reject you. If they persecuted Me they will persecute you. In many branches of the Church, the gospel is seen as *irrelevant* and changeable, and not acknowledged as primary to the fulfillment of the great commission. A comfortable gospel for a comfortable people is what is acceptable to many now. Something that doesn't *rock the proverbial* boat is preferred. Something that doesn't expect change or transformation from within.

2 Timothy 3:1-5 says *"But know this, that in the last days perilous times will come: men will be lovers of themselves, lovers of money, boasters, proud, blasphemers, disobedient to parents, unthankful, unholy, ³unloving, unforgiving, slanderers, without self-control, brutal, despisers of good, ⁴traitors, headstrong, haughty, lovers of pleasure rather than lovers of God, ⁵***having a form of godliness but denying its power****. And from such people turn away!"*

Luke 10:16 *"He who hears you hears Me, he who rejects you rejects Me, and he who rejects Me rejects Him who sent Me."*

John 15:20 *"Remember the word that I said to you, 'A servant is not greater than his master.'* ***If they persecuted Me, they*** *will also persecute you.* ***If they*** *kept My word,* ***they*** *will keep yours also."*

The issue of Jesus being hidden from the church, is all too often associated with rejecting the true mature apostle and prophets' ministry. To reject the apostolic prophetic heart of God, is to leave the Church with blinded eyes and deafened ears!

The principle stands true when we understand that we *get* what we *receive*. Matthew 10:41 says *"He who **receives a prophet** in the **name of a prophet** shall **receive a prophet's** reward. And he who receives a righteous man in the **name of a righteous man** shall **receive a righteous man's** reward."*

Familiarity is another issue that plays a part in whether or not we are able to receive the revelation that we need. We see this happening with Jesus and His family members.

John 7:4-5 *"⁴For no one does anything in secret while he himself seeks to be known openly. If You do these things, show Yourself to the world." ⁵**For even His brothers did not believe in Him.**"*

John 1:46 says concerning those who Knew Jesus as the carpenters son *"And Nathanael said to him,* **"Can anything good come out of Nazareth?"** *Philip said to him,* **"Come** *and see.""*

Mark 6:4 *"But Jesus said to them, "A **prophet** is **not without honour** except in his own country, among his own relatives, and in his own house."*

Familiarity often ends in rejection. This was demonstrated repeatedly in Jesus earthly life and ministry among the religious leaders and the Jews.

Peeling back the layers...... The apostles and prophets are peeling the onion. They are peeling back & removing the layers. Apostle Paul gives a good understanding and explanation of the apostolic prophetic heart of God in revealing Jesus.

Paul says it very well in Ephesians 3: 3-7 *"³how that by revelation He made known to me the mystery (as I have briefly written already, ⁴by which, when you read, you may understand my knowledge in the mystery of Christ), ⁵which in other ages was not made known to the sons of men,* **as it has now been revealed by the Spirit to His holy apostles and prophets:** *⁶that the Gentiles should be fellow heirs, of the same body, and partakers of His promise in Christ through the gospel, ⁷of which I became a minister according to the gift of the grace of God given to me by the effective working of His power."*

Paul warns us in Colossians 2:4-10 not to be deceived...."*⁸Beware lest anyone cheat you through philosophy and empty deceit, according to the tradition of men, according to the basic principles of the world, and not according to Christ.' ⁹For In Him dwells all the fullness of the Godhead bodily,¹⁰and you are complete in Him, who is the head of all principality and power."*

Both the church and the world needs to see Jesus. He is the manifest expression of Father God's heart. He is being made manifest through the apostolic prophetic heart of God in the apostle and prophet in this hour.

The apostolic prophetic heart of God must be able to influence and raise the sons and daughters of God so that they can pattern their lives after Christ, not the world, otherwise Christ will be hidden. It was the apostle Paul that said *"imitate me as I imitate Christ"* (1 Corinthians.11:1).

I wonder how many of us can say *"follow me as I follow Jesus", copy me as I copy Jesus, follow my example and you will see Jesus"*?

Apostle Paul's letter to the Colossians has a great admonition in it for us in chapter two. Many claim to have great revelation concerning Christ and spiritual things, and yet they have no real connection to Christ as the Head or to the members of the Church which is His body.

Colossians 2:18-19 "*¹⁸Let no one cheat you of your reward, taking delight in false humility and worship of angels, intruding into those things which he has not seen, vainly puffed up by his fleshly mind, ¹⁹and not holding fast to the Head, from whom all the body, nourished and knit together by joints and ligaments, grows with the increase that is from God."*

Let us pray that Jesus Christ is revealed in these last days unhindered, like never before! May those who seek Him with all their heart find Him, without deception leading them astray. May the risen, glorified

Lord Jesus Christ make Himself known to many potential sons and daughters of God.

Time is running out. May we not just know his doctrine but also His person through the Holy Spirit's revelatory work in our hearts and lives. For even the *spirit of prophecy* bears testimony to the risen and glorified Son of God, the Lord Jesus Christ (Rev. 19:10).

The apostle and prophet must lead the sons and daughters of God to the revelation of Jesus Christ. Spiritual fathers and mothers must reveal Jesus.

Let us pray that Jesus would not be hidden from those who are seeking answers and want to truly know Him. Let us be *revelators* of the person of the Lord Jesus Christ, as we seek God for the restoration of all things. Amen!

****
Matthew 16:16
*"Simon Peter answered and said, **"You are the Christ, the Son of the living God."***
****

CHAPTER EIGHT

Restoration Based on the Everlasting Covenant!

If we look at all of God's interaction with man since the beginning of creation and time, as recorded in the scriptures of the Holy Bible, we will see that God is a covenant making and covenant keeping God.
Some of the covenants that God has made with man are quite plain and explicit in their instructions and conditions, and others are a little more subtle. For those of us that understand that God is not a man that He should lie (Numbers 23:19), we also would understand that He has made covenants with his creation to reinforce and establish that unchanging truth concerning His character.

When one looks closely at the scriptures, one can safely say that God has made a covenant with every human vessel He has ever interacted with, throughout the course of history. Every man God made a covenant with was to be a *type* of father, a representative of his *Heavenly Father*, to the generation of sons and daughters he was to influence and lead. Those covenants were always designed and put in place by *Father God*, to steer His chosen *patriarchs* in the direction of righteousness, and an unbroken relationship with Him!

If we consider Adam the first man of the *dust of the earth* and son of God created in his image, he was told what he was *to do* and what he was *not to do*, to maintain a holy and acceptable relationship with God. This was a kind of covenant, an agreement, a contract. There were conditions, expectations and consequences.

The consequences of Adam breaking the covenant through his disobedience, resulted in broken fellowship/relationship, and being put out of the garden of Eden. As a result Spiritual death and physical death entered into the human condition, which the whole human race deals with today.

Then there was Noah the builder of the ark; whom God used (along with his family) to repopulate the earth after the Flood with a rainbow placed in the heavens signalling a covenant, to never again destroy the earth by flood because of man's wickedness (Genesis 9:11,17).

Then there was a covenant made with Abraham (Genesis 12:1-3, Genesis 17:4-5). But even before God made a covenant with Abraham, He made him a promise and swore by Himself. It says in Hebrews 6:13-14 *"For when God made a promise to Abraham, because He could swear by no one greater, He swore by Himself, [14] saying, "Surely blessing I will bless you, and multiplying I will multiply you."*

Covenant relationship continued in Isaac (Genesis 21:12, Genesis 22:17-18), and Jacob (Genesis 28:14-19). Then we see God making a covenant with Moses and the people of Israel with the laws and commandments being given (Exodus ch.19 & ch.24, Exodus 31:18, Deuteronomy ch.28 & ch.29). Covenant continues with Joshua (Joshua 8:30-35), David and the Davidic Covenant (2 Samuel 7:8-29), then through Solomon (1 Kings 9:3, 2 Chronicles 8) and all the way down through the passage of time in fulfillment of prophecy spoken by all the prophets to the promised messiah, redeemer, saviour, deliverer *JESUS CHRIST!* The covenant of all covenants. The covenant that fulfills all other covenants. The everlasting covenant.

All these men preceding the time of Christ, were to be fathers to their generations, with a responsibility to walk in covenant relationship with God and produce sons and daughters that would do the same.

Our God is a covenant keeping God as it says in Deuteronomy 7:9 *"Therefore know that the Lord your God, He is God, the faithful God who keeps covenant and mercy for a thousand generations with those who love Him and keep His commandments"*

An *everlasting covenant* is what God has always wanted. (Genesis 17:6,19, Jeremiah 32:40, 2 Samuel 23:5, Psalm 105:8, Isaiah 55:3.)

Restoration based on covenant relationship has always been part of God's plan. Let us consider the everlasting covenant:

Ezekiel 16:60-63 *"Nevertheless I will remember My covenant with you in the days of your youth,* **and I will establish an everlasting covenant with you.** *61 Then you will remember your ways and be ashamed, when you receive your older and your younger sisters; for I will give them to you for daughters, but not because of My covenant with you. 62 And I will establish My covenant with you. Then you shall know that I am the Lord, 63 that you may remember and be ashamed, and never open your mouth anymore because of your shame, when I provide you an atonement for all you have done," says the Lord God.'"*

Verse 61 speaks to us of remembering *our* ways and being ashamed. Verse 62 speaks to us of *knowing* God as *Lord*. Verse 63 speaks of God providing *atonement* for *all* we have *done*.

God has taken us from a covenant that brings guilt and a remembrance of sin and shame, to a covenant that removes sin, shame and guilt. God has taken us from a covenant that relied on our performance and understanding of His laws; to a covenant that empowers us and writes his laws upon our hearts by his Spirit.

As the writer states in...

Hebrews 10:15-16 *"¹⁵But the Holy Spirit also witnesses to us; for after He had said before,¹⁶"This is the covenant that I will make with them after those days, says the Lord:* **I will put My laws into their hearts, and in their minds I will write them,"**

2 Corinthians 3:3 *"clearly you are an epistle of Christ, ministered by us, written not with ink but* **by the Spirit of the living God, not on tablets of stone but on tablets of flesh, that is, of the heart."**

The patriarchal fathers and prophets of the old covenant, lived by and continually called the people back to a covenant, that could never deal with sin once and for all.

Just as God saw and spoke through the early patriarchs and prophets, as the fathers to the nation of Israel, I believe He also sees the apostles and prophets of the new covenant *in* Christ as the *spiritual* fathers and mothers to his people in the *ecclesia,* the called out ones, that is, *the Church.*

His apostles and prophets with the *apostolic prophetic heart of God,* are calling His people *through the gospel,* to walk in covenant relationship with Him, and each other! It is on the basis of His new and everlasting covenant, established through His only begotten Son, Jesus Christ.

Hebrews 13:20 says *"Now may the God of peace who brought up our Lord Jesus from the dead, that great Shepherd of the sheep, through the* **blood of the everlasting covenant,"**

When Jesus shared His last supper with the 12 disciples that He had appointed as apostles, he declared the cup which He shared; as representing the *blood of a new covenant.*

Luke 22:20 *"likewise He also took the cup after supper saying, This cup is the new covenant in My blood, which is shed for you."*

Apostle Paul echoes the Lord Jesus Christ in 1 Corinthians 11:25 when he says to the believers, *"In the same manner He also took the cup after supper, saying, "This cup is the new covenant in My blood. This do, as often as you drink it, in remembrance of Me."*

Hebrews 8:6-9 *"⁶But now He has obtained a more excellent ministry, in as much as, He is also Mediator of a better covenant, which was established on better promises."*

Based on the above verses of scripture, we see that the covenant that God has made with us in this Church/kingdom age is 1. New 2. Better & 3. Everlasting

Apostle Paul declares in his epistle to the Corinthians in 1 Cor.4:15-16 *"For though you might have ten thousand instructors in Christ, yet you do not have many fathers; for in Jesus Christ I have begotten you through the gospel. Therefore I urge you, imitate me."*

So now, we can also add a fourth component to the above three things, that is the role of the spiritual parent, the spiritual fathers and mothers. True spiritual fathers and mothers that walk with God and demonstrate covenant relationship, for the sons and daughters that will be revealed.

This means we must live in total commitment to God and each other, as well as walk in the light before God and each other based on the cup of the New Covenant which we drink from every time we share in communion.

Apostle John declares to the believers in 1 John 1:5-9 *"⁵his is the message which we have heard from Him and declare to you, that God is light and in Him there is no darkness at all." "⁶if we say that we have fellowship with Him, and walk in darkness, we lie and do not practice the truth. ⁷But if we walk in the light as He is in the light, we have fellowship with one another, and the blood of Jesus Christ His Son cleanses us from all sin. ⁸If we say that we have no sin, we deceive ourselves, and the truth is not in us. ⁹If we confess our sins, He is faithful and just to forgive us our sins and to cleanse us from all unrighteousness."*

True fellowship and forgiveness comes with walking in the light towards one another as well as with God. It is the blood of Christ that washes us and cleanses us. It is the blood of Christ that has made way for this everlasting covenant.

Ephesians 2:13 *"But now in Christ Jesus you who once were far off have been brought near by the blood of Christ."*

An Intimate walk / relationship with God should be the result. Not only spiritual fathers and mothers that truly know the heart of God the Fathers restoration, but also the sons and daughters that will be made ready to be revealed.

God's everlasting covenant has led us to, and joined us to, his grace by faith with an everlasting covenant at the foundation of the relationship!

Ephesians 2:8-10 *"⁸For by grace you have been saved through faith, and that not of yourselves; it is the gift of God, ⁹not of works, lest anyone should boast. ¹⁰For we are His workmanship, created in Christ Jesus for good works, which God prepared beforehand that we should walk in them."*

Those who know their God, shall reveal their God, as they do great exploits! They shall be for a sign and wonder that points to God's Restoration!

Daniel 11:32
"Those who do wickedly against the covenant he shall corrupt with

*flattery; but the people who know their God shall be strong, and carry out **great exploits**."*

The *revealing of the sons of God* (Romans 8:19) shall indeed take place in *the restoration of all things* (Acts 3:21), based on His *everlasting covenant*.

Jesus is received in Heaven until the restoration of all things. The apostolic prophetic heart of God at work by the Spirit, in His apostles and prophets shall indeed make room for the restoration and revealing of the sons and daughters of God.

Let us therefore not forget the following instruction and exhortation from:

2 Timothy 2:19 *"Nevertheless the solid foundation of God stands, having this seal: "The Lord knows those who are His," and, "Let everyone who names the name of Christ depart from iniquity."*

We are resting, waiting and working based on an everlasting covenant, that is part of the sure foundation of God. Hallelujah!

The birth pangs have started and have been happening for some time! All of creation is waiting. (Romans 8:18-22) Expectations are high. Let us not lose heart or grow weary in doing good.

The Holy Spirit, the Spirit of Adoption is at work in the sons and daughters of God!

****

1 Corinthians 11:25

*"In the same manner He also took the cup after supper, saying, **"This cup is the new covenant in My blood**. This do, as often as you drink it, in remembrance of Me."*

****

CHAPTER NINE

The Restoration of Foundations and a Cutting Edge!

Foundations are important. They are fundamental to the success and longevity of any great work or building. The righteous need good foundations to build on if they are going to pursue the purpose of God for their life or the lives of others.

Psalm 11:3 says *"If the foundations are destroyed, what can the righteous do?"* The Church of Jesus Christ must also have a good foundation.

The apostolic prophetic heart is given to the apostle and prophet, along with the other ascension gift ministries, to build and restore the foundations of God's family, the Church. The sons and daughters of God need good foundations along with every other member of the household of faith.

They understand and recognise the danger of building on sand and are always aware of the necessity to build upon the rock . They are always listening for the Master's word and will seek to execute it (Matthew 7:24-27).

They never forget that the Church is an express manifestation of the Kingdom of God in the earth. It has been given eternal foundations in the person of Jesus Christ the triumphant, victorious Son of God.

The Church was birthed by the Spirit of God on the day of Pentecost (Acts 2). It was and continues to be added to daily by the Spirit of God, as the gospel is preached.

1 Timothy 3:14-15 *"These things I write to you, though I hope to come to you shortly; [15] but if I am delayed, I write so that you may know how you ought to conduct yourself in the house of God, which is the church of the living God, the pillar and ground of the truth.*

In this passage, apostle Paul highlights the importance of the Church as the pillar and ground/foundation of the truth. Jesus himself declared that the gates of hell shall not prevail against it. The foundation of the Church is unshakable and unmistakable. Founded on the person who is the way, the truth, the life.

Two of the all-important functions of apostles and prophets is seen in the fact that they are essentially equipped by God to, 1. Parent and 2. Plant churches (God's family), not just individuals.

They carry the Father's apostolic prophetic heart. They see the church as the apple of Father God's eye! Always looking to impart a gift that equips and empowers. Encouraging growth that makes for the maturing and restoration of the sons and daughters of God. Laying foundations and the re-aligning of foundations are something they specialize in as well as fathering and mentoring ministries.

Hebrews 12:28-29 says, *"Therefore, since we are receiving a kingdom which can not be shaken, let us have grace, by which we may serve God acceptably with reverence and godly fear. [29] For our God is a consuming fire"*

1 Corinthians 3:13 *"each ones work will become clear; for the Day will declare it, because it will be revealed by fire, and the fire will test each one's work, of what sort it is."*

A part of the *restoration of all things* to Himself, means that He is restoring the:

1. The Foundations in an individual person's life.

2. The foundations in a corporate family.

3. The foundations in God's corporate (spiritual) family.

Hebrews 6:1-2 **speaks to us of the doctrinal foundations** and teaching of the Christian faith, which the apostolic prophetic heart of God builds on with Christ as the chief cornerstone.

1. *Repentance* from dead works.

2. *Faith* towards God.

3. Doctrine of **Baptisms**.

4. *Laying* on of hands.

5. *Resurrection* of the dead.

6. Eternal *judgment*.

Right foundations can't be shaken to the point of destruction. God's foundations can not be shaken at all. They are immovable. The apostolic prophetic heart of God facilitates the building of the foundations of God in peoples lives, both individually and corporately.

So much building has taken place on the sand producing wrong foundations seen in:

1. Worldly patterns and ways of doing things.

2. Formulas.

3. Worldly Philosophies.

4. Emphasising personality and charisma rather than Christ-centered character.

5. Mosaic centered, rather than Christ-centered, preaching & teaching.

1 Corinthians 3: 11- 13 *"For no other foundation can anyone lay than that which is laid, which is Jesus Christ. ^{12}Now if anyone builds on this foundation with gold, silver, precious stones, wood, hay, straw, ^{13}each one's work will become clear; for the Day will declare it, because it will be revealed by fire; and the fire will test each one's work, of what sort it is."*

Good and Solid Foundations that remain after the shaking and fiery trials and tests, are what God needs to build on.

Ephesians 2:19-20 *"Now, therefore, you are no longer strangers and foreigners, but fellow citizens with the saints and members of the household of God, ^{20}having been built on the foundations of the apostles and prophets, Jesus Christ Himself being the chief cornerstone."*

Apostles and prophets are God's foundation layers as well as God's parents, the spiritual fathers and mothers to the Church that built and plant with gold, silver and precious stones, not hay wood and stubble!

It could be said that two things are needed for a healthy Church family to survive and thrive:

1. *Good planting* and good foundations individually and corporately.

2. *Good parenting* brings good healthy growth and maturity individually and corporately

The apostolic and the prophetic gifts of God can discern God's shaking of the foundations and help bring correction and adjustment.

Foundationally speaking, and for the growth of a local fellowship, the book of Acts shows us the divine pattern of apostles and prophets *appointing* or setting *elders* in place.

Acts 14:23 says of Paul and Barnabas, *"So when they had appointed elders in every church, and prayed with fasting, they commended them to the Lord in whom they believed."*

On occasions the apostles and prophets sent an apostolic delegate to set things in order and appoint elders as seen in Titus 1:5 *"For this reason I left you in Crete, that you should set in order the things that are lacking, and appoint elders in every city as I commanded you"*

We see here that apostle Paul had delegated the responsibility to Titus, to set things in order and appoint elders through out the towns and cities in Crete.

Titus was entrusted with the responsibility that flows from the apostolic prophetic heart, given to Paul by God for the benefit and health of the Church in Crete. The mature apostolic prophetic heart becomes a wise master builder, in partnership with Father God whether in foundation laying, building or spiritual warfare.

1 Corinthians 3:10-11 says *"[10] According to the grace of God which was given to me, as a wise master builder I have laid the foundation, and another builds on it. But let each one take heed how he builds on it. [11] For no other foundation can anyone lay than that which is laid, which is Jesus Christ."*

1 Timothy 1:18 says *"18 This charge I commit to you, son Timothy, according to the prophecies previously made concerning you, that by them you may wage the good warfare,"*

Dismantling, Planting, Restoring!

God is dismantling the ways of man and restoring paths of righteousness for man to walk in. Hence the need for the apostolic and prophetic heart of God in the apostle and prophet. They are given supernatural wisdom and discernment to partner with God in growing His family. They understand the application of the quickened word and the workings of the Spirit to produce fruit. (Hebrews.4: 12, Galatians 5:22-26)

On the 6th and 7th of February in 1994, I remember coming to the end of an extended fast that the Lord had directed me to go on. At this time he was speaking to me about my calling to ministry and Christian service. He led me to the book of Jeremiah in the Old Testament.

He specifically took me to Jeremiah 1:9-10… where it says… *9"Then the Lord put forth His hand and touched my mouth, and the Lord said to me: "Behold I have put my words in your mouth. 10See, I have this day set you over the nations and over the kingdoms, To root out and to pull down, To destroy and to throw down, To build and to plant."*

The Lord at this time was speaking to me; not only about my calling, but also about the apostolic prophetic heart and the function that these father heart ministries would carry out. Sometimes an *uprooting* must take place before there can be a *planting*. Sometimes there must be a demolishing or *dismantling* before there can be a *building*. At certain times and seasons there needs to be some pruning done before there can be further growth.

I remember back in June of 1998 sitting in my study to prepare for a meeting. The Lord began to speak to me about the *dismantling* of certain aspects of His church. He told me that He wanted a *corporate*

Son, that is, His Church, His Body, His family that would reflect His Character. That which would demonstrate His Function and His Purpose in the earth. A church that would look just like His Son Jesus. He told me he was going to begin dismantling certain church leadership structures and some of the ways man was running His church. He told me that he wanted a relationship-centered family, with a Christ-centered message being preached rather than a mosaic or law centered gospel. He told me that titles and *corporate world patterns* were not the way of His family. He told me that programs were no longer to be relied upon for true spiritual life and growth.

An Axe head and a Cutting Edge!

Apostles and prophets are the fathers and mothers that God is giving to the Church as a *cutting edge* like sharpened axe heads. They can help restore the cutting edge in others. They equip the sons and daughters, giving them a cutting edge to answer the call.

An axe head, a cutting edge, is needed to build on the restored foundations.

In 2 Kings 6:1-7 we read about one of the sons of the prophets losing his borrowed axe head in the water. Without it he could not chop the trees down.

2 Kings 6:5 *"But as one was cutting down a tree, the iron ax head fell into the water; and he cried out and said, "Alas, master! For it was borrowed.""*

The prophet Elisha, who was as a master and father to the *sons of the prophets*, was called upon to help retrieve the axe head. The prophet helped him get his cutting edge back; to do the job he was meant to do.

The apostles and prophets help bring God the Father's *cutting edge* for making preparation for restoration. Matthew 3:10 and Luke 3:9 show us the kind of apostolic prophetic heart and ministry that John the Baptist had been trained and prepared for:

Matthew 3:10 *"And even now the ax is laid to the root of the trees. Therefore every tree which does not bear good fruit is cut down and thrown into the fire."*

John the Baptist was the cousin of Jesus, but as a prophet of God and a forerunner to the Saviour, he was given the right heart attitude and state of mind for the season. He was trained and raised in the back side of the desert; to be able to rebuke and challenge the dry religious leaders of the day.

He had the much needed cutting edge for the circumstances he faced, to prepare the foundations needed and fulfill the purpose of the Father, in making way for Jesus.

In 1 Samuel 13:19-23 we read of a situation in which the Israelite's had no weapons of warfare for the day of battle against the Philistines, in fact the scripture says that there was no spear, no sword, in the hands of God's people on the day of battle. Only Saul and Jonathon had a weapon:

[19]*Now there was no blacksmith to be found throughout all the land of Israel, for the Philistines said, "Lest the Hebrews make swords or spears."* [20]*But all the Israelites would go down to the Philistines to sharpen each man's plowshare, his mattock, his ax, and his sickle;* [21]*and the charge for a sharpening was a pim for the plowshares, the mattocks, the forks, and the axes, and to set the points of the goads.* [22]*So it came about, on the day of battle, that there was* **neither sword nor spear found in the hand** *of any of the people who were with Saul and Jonathan. But they were found with Saul and Jonathan his son."*

All of God's sons and daughters need to be equipped with a cutting edge. Some have lost their cutting edge and need to have it restored back to them!

Yet another illustration we can draw from allegorically in scripture, is found in Nehemiah 4:17. *"Those who built on the wall, and those who carried burdens, loaded themselves so that with one hand they worked at construction, and with the other held a weapon."*

Here we see the walls of Jerusalem being built. The scripture tells us that they built the walls as they fought the enemy. They had a *sword* in one hand and a *trowel* in the other.

The apostle and prophet, in God's hands, are His instruments to build and warfare. They are to train and equip the people of God. As David says in Psalm 144:1 *"Blessed be the Lord my Rock, who trains my hands for war, and my fingers for battle"*

If there are No apostles and prophets, there can be No Cutting edge, No Axe head, No Sickle.

Apostles and prophets have always been part of God's plan for Restoration. They are the fathers and mothers that prepare the way; for the sons and daughters of God to walk in.

Apostles and prophets are God's cutting edge restorers. The restorers of paths to dwell in. (Isaiah 58:12) The *repairers* of the breach. The *re-connectors* and *re-joiners* of the breaks and tears in *His body, His Church*, the *menders* of the net. Just like a piece of cloth or fabric that needs mending.

Sometimes God's fathers and mothers, that is His apostles and prophets, come with a spiritual tool box that has in it a variety of tools, with just the right measure of grace given by the Lord Jesus; to use them according to the task or challenge at hand.

Sometimes they contain *surgical type* instruments (metaphorically speaking) for precision and accuracy in dealing with whatever the situation! Other times they contain hammers, chisels and screwdrivers for the tougher jobs.

The tools in the spiritual tool box, that the spirit of God supplies to the apostle and prophet can be compared to:

1. *A Pick, shovel or rake.* They need to choose the right tool for the job.

2. *A needle and thread.* To fix tears and do repairs.

3. *A Stethoscope.* For listening to the individual person's heart or the corporate Church's heart: (Examples: Matt.13:1-9 and 18-23-parable of the Sower or the Church family's heart. Revelation Ch's 2 and 3. Representing: Seven- *corporate body* heart conditions.

As apostle Paul says in Romans 1:11 *"For I long to see you, that I may impart to you some spiritual gift, so that you may be established"*

Hebrews 12:12-13 say's *"Therefore strengthen the hands which hang down, and the feeble knees, ¹³and make straight paths for your feet, so that what is lame may not be dislocated, but rather be healed."*

The apostolic prophetic heart is given the grace to be a wise master builder (1 Corinthians 3:10) and therefore can bring strength and wholeness and healing into the weaker parts of the body, restoring paths of righteousness to dwell in.

Isaiah 58:12 *"Those from among you shall build the old waste places; You shall raise up the foundations of many generations; and you shall be called the Repairer of the Breach, The Restorer of Streets to Dwell In."*

1 Corinthians 3:9 tells us that they are God's *fellow workers* and they are appointed by God to work in *His fields*. It also tells us that they are appointed to work on *God's building* of which we are all a part.

The apostolic prophetic heart of God has within it what is needed, to not only prepare the foundation, but also to be able to build on it!

Let us pray for our *Kingdom of God foundation layers and builders* that they will have the wisdom and insight to fulfill the great commission in restoring and building on the right foundations, as they equip the sons and daughters of God. Amen!

***

1 Corinthians 3:10
*"According to the grace of God which was given to me, as a **wise master builder** I have laid the foundation, and another builds on it. But let each one take heed how he builds on it."*

***

CHAPTER TEN

Restoration of Inheritance, Gifts and Callings!

The Restoration Of Inheritance

Romans 8:16-17 says, *"¹⁶The Spirit Himself bears witness with our spirit that we are **children of God**, ¹⁷and if children, then heirs—**heirs of God and joint heirs with Christ**, if indeed we suffer with Him, that we may also be glorified together."*

The divine pattern of fatherhood and sonship brings with it the restoration of inheritance,

1. Inheritance is *restored* when we understand and *reclaim* our birthright.

2. Sons and daughters have an Inheritance by *birthright*.

3. Sons and daughters have an inheritance as their *possession*.

4. *Servants* do not have an *Inheritance* by birthright.

5. There is a restoration of *Inheritance* happening *spiritually and materially*.

Ezekiel 46:16-18 *"¹⁶Thus says the Lord God: "if the prince gives a gift of some of his inheritance to any of his son's, it shall belong to his son's; it is their possession by inheritance. ¹⁷But if he gives a gift of some of his inheritance to one of his servants, it shall be his until the year of liberty; after which it shall return to the prince. But his inheritance shall belong to his sons; it shall become theirs."*

Romans 8:17 says *"and if children, then heirs—heirs of God and joint heirs with Christ....."*

We are children of God, therefore we are heirs- heirs of God and joint heirs with Christ.

Hebrews 6: 12 says *"that you do not become sluggish but imitate those who through faith & patience inherit the promises."*

One of the greatest things that can happen in a Christian's life is when they find and can enter into a relationship, with a spiritual father or mother as a true son or daughter!

If they can stay the distance in the relationship, they will receive of the apostolic prophetic heart that is within the father or mother. This is the path to receiving one of the greatest forms of inheritance that a son or daughter can receive. What am I talking about? I am talking about receiving an inheritance in the form of an anointing, a mantle, a ministry.

The passing on and the increasing of what was in the spiritual father or mother, is found in the son or daughter who has the heart, the mind, and more importantly the spiritual capacity. Spiritual inheritance is more important than any other form of inheritance. It is the heart of God being carried and passed from one generation to another! What is passed on is often caught more than it is taught, and requires the son, the daughter to be there right to the end of the race, that God has planned for them.

2 Kings 2:9-10 "⁹And so it was, when they had crossed over, that Elijah said to Elisha, "Ask! What may I do for you, before I am taken away from you?" Elisha said, "Please let a double portion of your spirit be upon me." ¹⁰So he said, "You have asked a hard thing. Nevertheless, if you see me when I am taken from you, it shall be so for you; but if not, it shall not be so.""

Faithfulness to a spiritual father or mother and perseverance in learning the lessons is what makes way for receiving an enlarged spiritual inheritance. This is what we see in the life of Elisha as he received from Elijah right at the end of the prophet and spiritual father's race. Increase is seen in the double-portion anointing that Elisha received, and was made manifest through the many miracles that doubled what Elijah had done, in his ministry as a prophet.

If we look at the life of Joshua, we see that he had been Moses assistant (Exodus 24:13, Numbers 11:28) for a long time, for at least 40 years in the wilderness. Joshua was the young man that was like a son to Moses that was always there in the background. Faithful and serving as a son. He lingered outside the entry of the tabernacle. Even after Moses had left the tabernacle, Joshua would not depart (Exodus 33:11). Joshua desired what he saw in the man that was like a father to him. Moses as a Father to Joshua and the nation of Israel, carried a sense of the weighty presence of God. By association as a son, Joshua received a great impartation from Moses.

It's worth noting that Joshua's material inheritance was connected to his spiritual inheritance. Deuteronomy 34:9 *"Now Joshua the son of Nun was full of the spirit of wisdom, for **Moses** had **laid his hands** on him; so the children of Israel heeded him, and did as the Lord had commanded **Moses**"*

Joshua 1:1-2 *"After the death of Moses the servant of the Lord, it came to pass that the Lord spoke to Joshua the son of Nun, Moses' assistant, saying: ²"Moses My servant is dead. Now therefore, arise, go over this Jordan, you and all this people, to the land which I am giving to them—the children of Israel."*

Joshua, in taking up His spiritual inheritance through the laying of Moses hands, was also taking hold of what would be his material inheritance. That is his allotted piece of land; in the promised land, along with his tribe. Joshua's desire to possess his spiritual inheritance meant the fulfillment of his associated responsibility, as the newly appointed leader of Israel. This made way for others to possess, not only their spiritual inheritance but also their allotted material inheritance in the promised land.

If we consider yet another example found in the life of the patriarch Jacob (Israel), we will see that Jacob desired so much, the birthright of inheritance. Not only did he want the birthright of inheritance, but he wanted what customarily belonged to the oldest son! Along with his mother Rebekah, he employed a plan based on deception to get from his father the ultimate prophetic blessing and inheritance (Genesis 25:29-34).

We know from reading the scripture (Genesis 25:23-27) that God had spoken to Rebekah about Esau and Jacob, whilst they were still in her womb. We can say the prophetic word as per the heart of God, was pushing for the fulfillment of the word in Rebekah and Jacob.

The apostolic prophetic heart was connected to and driving the fulfillment of God's word and the birthright of inheritance in both mother and son. One wonders what might have happened, if it had not been done deceptively.

Let us not forget that every child of God in this *dispensation of grace* that we are in right now, has an inheritance that is connected to the prophetic fulfillment of God's word in their life.

As a new creation in Christ, we should seek to become a true son or daughter and discover our God given destiny and purpose! This demands that we accept our birthright and the responsibility that goes with it!

Our Heavenly Father provides for all our needs according to His riches in glory by Christ Jesus (Philippians 4:19) Every son and daughter of God has an inheritance! May the apostolic prophetic heart of God help them connect with their inheritance and possess it.

Restoration of Gifts and Callings

2 Corinthians 4:7 *"But we have this **treasure in earthen vessels**, that the excellence of the power may be of God and not of us."*

The apostolic prophetic heart of God searches out the treasure in the earthen vessel and seeks to put it to use, in preaching the gospel and extending the rule of the kingdom of God into the hearts of others.

The divine pattern seen in Fatherhood and sonship makes way for this to happen.

1 Peter 4:10 says *"As each one has received a gift, minister it to one another, as good stewards of the manifold grace of God."*

Revelation 1:6 *"and has made us to be a kingdom and priests to serve his God and Father—to him be glory and power for ever and ever! Amen."*

Many gifts and callings have laid dormant for a long time. Many gifts and callings have had dung heaped on top of them. They have been buried and need to be unearthed.

Many gifts and callings have been twisted and distorted by man. Man's teachings, man's ways, working from a natural or carnal platform rather than a spiritual platform.

So many gifts and callings have been buried, underneath sin, shame, unforgiveness, bitterness, control, manipulation, confusion, ungodly and wrong structures etc. The scripture says in Romans 11:29 *"For the gifts and the calling of God are irrevocable."*

The uncovering, the discovering, the releasing of such gifts is in part what the *restoration of all things* unto Himself is all about. The apostolic prophetic gifts are God's key to unlock what is needed in this hour. They have a central role to play in this aspect of the restoration of all things. These are the fathers and mothers that God will use to discover and uncover the gifts and callings of God in an individual's life.

Many of God's sons and daughter have been running in the wrong lane for too long. Occupying the wrong space, the wrong position. This then causes others to stand in the wrong place, run in the wrong lane and try to function in ways they are not called to function. The *gifts given by God* are the tools and resources given to fulfill His eternal purpose in the earth!

The apostolic prophetic heart of God, within the apostle and prophet, is what is needed for the sons and daughters to be brought to a place of greater maturity and understanding. Being equipped and released by *real* spiritual fathers and mothers. The principle holds true in both the natural as well as the spiritual. For too long the family of God has been subjected to teaching and instruction that lacks the necessary impartation of a father or mother in the faith. Evangelists, Pastors and Teachers are able to do much but they can't do what only the apostle and prophet can do!
We are now living in a day where we have more Bible Schools and Bible Colleges than we have ever had, but we lack the fathers and mothers

that will walk with, and come alongside those who are being raised as sons and daughters! This is a modern day echo of Paul's words in:

1 Corinthians 4:15 *"For though you might have ten thousand **instructors in Christ**, yet you do not have **many** fathers; for **in Christ** Jesus I have begotten you through the gospel."*

Divorce is a practical illustration that demonstrates very well, what can sometimes happen to the gifts and callings of God in a person's life, as follows.....

For many their walk with God has been or become like a man or a woman with children who is now divorced. When a person goes through a divorce they are no longer married which means they are no longer a husband or wife. The relationship has ended but they are still a parent.

In this Illustration the responsibility of fatherhood or motherhood remains but the person is now disconnected from what is now their ex-marriage partner.

This typifies what happens to our gifts and callings with God. Because they are irrevocable they remain.

-The Gift Remains.

-The Call Remains.

-The Responsibility Remains.

-The Burden Remains.

When a divorce takes place there is a breaking of a covenant relationship. So it is also, when one is disconnected in relationship from God. Our relationship with God is based on the blood of His everlasting covenant.

To use the gifts and exercise the calling in the right way, one must be in right and unbroken relationship, with their Heavenly Father.

John 15:1-5 says *"I am the true vine, and My Father is the vine dresser. ²Every branch in Me that does not bear fruit He takes away; and every branch that bears fruit He prunes, that it may bear more fruit. ³You are already clean because of the word which I have spoken to you.⁴Abide in Me, and I in you. As the branch cannot bear fruit of itself, unless it abides in the vine, neither can you, unless you abide in Me. ⁵"I am the vine, you are the branches. He who abides in Me, and I in him, bears much fruit; for without Me you can do nothing."*

It is difficult, if not impossible, to exercise the gift, the call, or to carry the burden of responsibility, in a state of separation, divorce, disconnection or broken relationship. The result is that it ends up either buried, abandoned or misused and abused, But still the gift or call remains. The answer is we need to re-connect. The apostolic prophetic heart of God helps to do this in the restoration process. A reconciliation with God is what needs to happen as part of the restoration.

Reconnecting is about establishing or re-establishing relationship. Reconnecting to the vine. Jesus said apart from me you can do nothing (John 15: 1-5). Jesus said I am the vine you are the branches. A branch detached from the vine can not bear fruit. We can not exercise our gift and calling outside of being connected in relationship with God and His family.

Within the context of relationship there is accountability, responsibility, mutual recognition of calling and gifting. It makes way for the gift and call of God to produce fruit. It means the son or daughter of God can function as a part of God's family (the Church).

The apostolic prophetic heart of God is instrumentally at work through the apostle and prophet to achieve this outcome.

Acts 9:26-28 *"²⁶And when Saul had come to Jerusalem, he tried to join the disciples; but they were all afraid of him, and did not believe that he was a disciple. ²⁷But Barnabas took him and brought him to the apostles. And he declared to them how he had seen the Lord on the road, and that He had spoken to him, and how he had preached boldly at Damascus in the name of Jesus. ²⁸So he was with them at Jerusalem, coming in and going out."*

Barnabas is a good example of one having the apostolic prophetic heart of God. He could see in Paul at that stage what others couldn't see. He took Paul and introduced him to the other apostles in Jerusalem, after his Damascus road encounter with the risen Christ. Many feared Saul, the *now* converted Paul. He had done much harm to the church of Jesus Christ through his religious zealotry. He had commissioned the martyrdom of Stephen and struck much fear in the hearts of so many of the believers.

Paul eventually demonstrated the apostolic prophetic heart of God as a spiritual father, when he sent for John Mark later on in his ministry. On a previous occasion John Mark had failed to continue on in a mission with Paul and Barnabas and turned back from them in Pamphylia. As a result there came a separation between them. Paul and Silas continued on, and Barnabas left with John Mark and sailed to Cyprus.

Acts 15:36-41 *"³⁶Then after some days Paul said to Barnabas, "Let us now go back and visit our brethren in every city where we have preached the word of the Lord, and see how they are doing." ³⁷Now Barnabas was determined to take with them John called Mark. ³⁸But Paul insisted that they should not take with them the one who had departed from them in Pamphylia, and had not gone with them to the work. ³⁹Then the contention became so sharp that they parted from one another. And so Barnabas took Mark and sailed to Cyprus; ⁴⁰but Paul chose Silas and departed, being commended by the brethren to the grace of God. ⁴¹And he went through Syria and Cilicia, strengthening the churches."*

2 Timothy 4:11 *"Only Luke is with me. Get (John) Mark and bring him with you, for he is useful to me for ministry."* Such was the outworking of the apostolic prophetic heart of God, that was made evident in the apostle with a heart of restoration given by our Heavenly Father.

The gift and calling of God could not remain unused or without being exercised in and through John Mark's life. It took a father to see it. It took a father to empower and activate that gift and encourage that calling!

Sometimes it is, a stirring up of the gift that needs to take place. As Paul says in 2 Timothy 1:6 *"Therefore I remind you to **stir up the gift** of God which is in you through the laying on of my hands."* Like fanning the coals of a fire into a flame!

Let us be ever mindful and praying for those, who have personal struggles and don't see in themselves the potential that God our Father may allow us to see, as one of those with the apostolic prophetic heart of God.

You may just be the person God has chosen to help unearth, encourage, mentor and activate or re-activate the gift!

Father we thank you that your gifts and callings are irrevocable. Amen!

****

Ephesians 1:17-18

*"[17]that the God of our Lord Jesus Christ, the Father of glory, may give to you the spirit of wisdom and revelation in the knowledge of Him, [18]**the eyes of your understanding being enlightened; that you may know what is the hope of His calling, what are the riches of the glory of His inheritance in the saints,**[19] and what is the exceeding greatness of His power toward us who believe, according to the working of His mighty power"*

****

CHAPTER ELEVEN

Restoration of Unity and Grace!

Restoration of Unity

The restoration of unity is the power of *one* at work! Jesus said it well when He said, a house divided against itself won't stand (Mark 3:25, Matthew 12:25).

In Deuteronomy 6:4 it says, *"Hear, O Israel: The Lord our God, the Lord is one!"* There is unity in the Godhead, that is Father, Son and Holy Spirit. Three persons, one God.

All unity flows from God. There is no comparison, no competition, no striving, nothing to pull them apart within the Godhead. Therefore, no division, no disunity, no separation!

The ascension gift ministries of apostle, prophet, evangelist, pastor and teacher must all aim for and work towards the restoration of unity. But the apostolic prophetic heart of God working through the ministry of the apostle and prophet, as father's producing sons; will do this the best as mature spiritual parents. Their role and function is key to all the other ascension gift ministries being effective.

The ascension gift ministries are all given to the Church by Christ. They all flow out of Christ. Ephesians 4:11 *"And **He Himself gave** some to be apostles, some prophets, some evangelists, and some pastors and teachers"*

One Lord and five ascension gifts. Jesus of course stood in all of the ascension gift ministries. Just as one hand on the human body has four fingers and one thumb, they are all joined and made one, working together to form the hand and its associated functions. This also paints for us a picture of relationship between all the ascension gift ministries. Each finger and the thumb serves the purpose of the *whole*. The common purpose being to train, equip and bring to maturity the members of the body of Christ for service.

The gifts don't flow out of division or disunity, they proceed and are given out of oneness in the Godhead! Just as the spiritual manifestation gifts also flow from the working of the one Spirit. As it says in 1 Corinthians 12:4 *"There are diversities of gifts, but the same Spirit."*

While Paul was in Miletus, he sent to Ephesus for the elders (Acts 20:17-38). The elders he sent for, were elders to the various gatherings and fellowships of God's people. But apostle Paul saw them all as *one church* spread across the city, meeting in various locations. Not *many* churches but rather *one* church. One family of God. Many elders all joined in the Spirit. One purpose, one heart and of one mind, the mind of Christ. *Oneness* as opposed to division/segregation. No room for pride and selfishness! No room for thinking of ones self as higher than others. Sober judgment, humility, faithfulness and the sacrificial love of Christ motivating those serving in the eldership.

Paul's decision to call all the elders together at the time of his departure, was a strategy in itself to encourage unity among the shepherds of the flocks and at the same time warn against division and destruction from within. Apostle Paul knew very well that division would come on two fronts:

1. The flesh (1 John 2:15-16, Galatians 5:19-21).

2. The spirit realm where strong holds, principalities and powers operate (2 Corinthians 10:1-6, Ephesians 6:12).

Romans 12:3-6 says *"For I say, through the grace given to me, to everyone who is among you, not to think of himself more highly than he ought to think, but to think soberly, as God has dealt to each one a measure of faith. ⁴For as we have many members in one body, but all the members do not have the same function, ⁵so we, being many, are one body in Christ, and individually members of one another. ⁶Having then gifts differing according to the grace that is given to us..."*

Unity is required if we are to fully appreciate the fellowship of the mystery as apostle Paul calls it, in Ephesians 3:9. *"and to make all see what is the fellowship of the mystery, which from the beginning of the ages has been hidden in God who created all things through Jesus Christ;"*

Unity found in diversity is also something we must learn to appreciate. This is part of the multi-faceted expression of His family, His church that Paul refers to in Ephesians 3:10-11 *"¹⁰to the intent that now the* **manifold wisdom of God** *might be* **made known** *by the church to the principalities and powers in the heavenly places, ¹¹according to the eternal purpose which He accomplished in Christ Jesus our Lord,"*

In Ephesians 4:1-6 Paul speaks of *one body, one faith, one baptism, one God* and *Father of all* . One is the key to blessing. There is unity in the Godhead and so there needs to be in *His body.* *"³endeavouring to keep the unity of the Spirit in the bond of peace. ⁴There is one body and one Spirit, just as you were called in one hope of your calling; ⁵one Lord, one faith, one baptism; ⁶one God and Father of all, who is above all, and through all, and in you all."*

Jesus High Priestly prayer, as it is often referred to in John chapter 17, refers to the cry and intercession of Christ's heart, that we would be *one* even as He and the Father are one. In John 17:20-23 says, [20]*"I do not pray for these alone, but also for those who will believe in Me through their word;* [21]*that they all may be one, as You, Father, are in Me, and I in You; that they also may be one in Us, that the world may believe that You sent Me.* [22] *And the glory which You gave Me I have given them, that they may be one just as We are one:* [23]*I in them, and You in Me; that they may be made perfect in one, and that the world may know that You have sent Me, and have loved them as You have loved Me."*

Jesus was like a father to the 12 disciples. John 14:7 *"If you had known Me, you would have known My* **Father** *also; and from now on you know Him and have* **seen** *Him."*

John 14:9 *"Jesus said to him, "Have I been with you so long, and yet you have not known Me, Philip? He who has* **seen** *Me has* **seen the Father**; *so how can you say, 'Show us* **the Father***'?* Fathers and mothers look to see the sons and daughters as one in the family of God.

Psalm 133 tells us that God commands His blessing where there is unity.

"Behold, how good and how pleasant it is for brethren to dwell together in unity! [2]*It is like the precious oil upon the head, running down on the beard, the beard of Aaron, running down on the edge of his garments.* [3]*It is like the dew of Hermon, descending upon the mountains of Zion; for there the Lord commanded the blessing—Life forevermore."*

It is the *corporate* family anointing that becomes most powerful. The anointing that comes with unity is a powerful anointing! God's Family must come to unity. Unity of *the faith* and unity in the *Spirit*. This will make way for unity in the family of God. Unity among the sons and daughters of God. This will bring God's commanded blessing. A Glorious Triumphant Church with God's commanded blessing will be unstoppable.

A crucified life, lifestyle purity, doctrinal purity and purity of purpose that is singularly focused on preaching the gospel and teaching the apostles doctrine, are all necessary to facilitate *unity of the faith* and *unity of the Spirit*.

Acts 2:42-47 *"⁴²And they continued steadfastly in the apostles' doctrine and fellowship, in the breaking of bread, and in prayers. ⁴³Then fear came upon every soul, and many wonders and signs were done through the apostles. ⁴⁴Now all who believed were together, and had all things in common, ⁴⁵and sold their possessions and goods, and divided them among all, as anyone had need. ⁴⁶So continuing daily with one accord in the temple, and breaking bread from house to house, they ate their food with gladness and simplicity of heart, ⁴⁷praising God and having favor with all the people. And the Lord added to the church daily those who were being saved."*

On the Day of Pentecost, following the outpouring of the Holy Spirit in Jerusalem and the thousands that were added to the Church, the scriptures tells us that the believers continued in:

1. The Apostles Doctrine

2. Fellowship

3. Breaking of bread (communion)

4. Had all (material) things in common.

5. Met daily in the temple and from house to house. (publicly and house to house)

6. Praising and Worshipping God.

These were the non-negotiable's that kept the church unified in practice and demonstration of the Lord's power.

As apostle Paul tells his son, in the faith, Timothy in 1 Timothy 4:16 *"Take heed to yourself and to the doctrine. Continue in them, for in doing this you will save both yourself and those who hear you."*

In verse 3 of Jude's epistle we read of a *common salvation,* **not** each one devising their own plan for salvation. Their was a contending for *the faith* which was *once for all delivered to the saints.*

Jude *"³Beloved, while I was very diligent to write to you concerning our* **common salvation,** *I found it necessary to write to you exhorting you* **to contend earnestly for the faith which was once for all delivered to the saints."**

There was not *many gospels* and *many faiths* or *many different doctrines* concerning Christ *delivered* to the saints, but rather there was and should still be *one faith*, lending itself to *unity of the faith.*

Jude verse 4 goes on to say, *"⁴For certain men have crept in unnoticed, who long ago were marked out for this condemnation, ungodly men, who turn the grace of our God into lewdness and deny the only Lord God and our Lord Jesus Christ."*

Bad doctrine brings division and bad lifestyle separates, and also causes division and break down of the body of Christ. Both destroy unity of the faith and unity of the Spirit! The purity of the church is lost through such means.

Jesus warned of the leaven, that is the teaching/doctrine of the Pharisees and Sadducees spoiling and leading astray (Matthew 16:5-12). So too, must the apostles and prophets of today beware. They have been given the apostolic prophetic heart of God to father and mother the sons and daughters of God. It should be Christ and Christ alone! Is it any wonder that apostle Paul said I preach Christ and Him crucified? (1 Corinthians 1:23-30 & 1 Corinthians 2:2)

As apostle Paul says in 2 Corinthians 11:2 -4
*"For I am jealous for **you** with godly jealousy. For I have betrothed **you to** one husband, that I may **present you** as a chaste virgin **to Christ**.³But I fear, lest somehow, as the serpent deceived Eve by his craftiness, so your minds may be corrupted from the simplicity that is in Christ. ⁴For if he who comes preaches another Jesus whom we have not preached, or if you receive a different spirit which you have not received, or a different gospel which you have not accepted—you may well put up with it!"*

The apostolic prophetic heart of God is concerned about the purity of heart, doctrine and lifestyle of the sons and daughters of God. A father or mother in the faith with an undivided heart will produce sons and daughters in the faith with undivided hearts. They will lead the sons and daughters to Christ not themselves. They won't lead them to their own personality centered ideas, but rather to the person of Christ, the way the truth and the life; in everything.

In Galatians 1:6-9 Paul highlights the issue of those who turn away from Him so easily. Those who were called in the grace of Christ, but turn away because of another gospel or another Jesus being preached. Paul challenges this issue so strongly that he says in verse ⁸*"But even if we, or an angel from heaven, preach any other gospel to you than what we have preached to you, let him be accursed"* the word *accursed* is a strong word. The anglicised Greek word for *accursed* is *anathema* which means to be despised, shunned or vehemently disliked.

Paul knew very well the destructive result of bad doctrine, another gospel, another Jesus being taught. One of which is *a breaking* of unity!

A Glorious Triumphant Church with God's commanded blessing on the sons of God will be a great witness to the world and the Devil. Unity in the faith and unity in the Spirit, along with an uncompromising heart and lifestyle in the sons and daughters of God, will make way for great restoration and the revealing of the sons of God.

Restoration of Grace

2 Corinthians 4:13-15 *"And since we have the same spirit of faith, according to what is written, "I believed and therefore I spoke," we also believe and therefore speak, ^{14}knowing that He who raised up the Lord Jesus will also raise us up with Jesus, and will present us with you. ^{15}For all things are for your sakes,* **that grace, having spread through the many**, *may cause thanksgiving to abound to the glory of God."*

The grace that spreads through the many needs to be facilitated by his Fathers and mothers, His apostles and prophets. The role of Grace can be seen in the process of restoration. Without Grace there can be no restoration. The ascension gift ministries are to restore grace, especially his apostles and prophets with the apostolic prophetic heart of God which is a grace filled heart.

Grace prepares the way for:

Repentance - Romans 2:4 *"Or do you despise the riches of His goodness, forbearance, and long suffering, not knowing that the goodness of God leads you to repentance?"*

Forgiveness - Psalm 103:1-4 *"Bless the Lord, O my soul; And all that is within me, bless His holy name! ^{2}Bless the Lord, O my soul, And forget not all His benefits:*
^{3} Who forgives all your iniquities, Who heals all your diseases,
^{4} Who redeems your life from destruction, Who crowns you with lovingkindness and tender mercies"

Rebuilding. - Isaiah 58:12 *"Those from among you shall build the old waste places; You shall raise up the foundations of many generations; and* *you shall be called the Repairer of the Breach, the Restorer of Streets to Dwell In"*

Re-Establishing - 1 Peter 5:10 *"But may the God of all grace, who called us to His eternal glory by Christ Jesus, after you have suffered a while, **perfect, establish,** strengthen, and **settle** you."*

Paths of righteousness to walk in - Psalm 23:3 *"He restores my soul; He leads me in the paths of righteousness for His name's sake.*

Restores the ancient paths - Jeremiah 6:16 *"Stand in the ways and see, "And ask for the old paths, where the good way is, And walk in it; Then you will find rest for your souls. But they said, 'We will not walk in it.'"*

Grace opens the way for family and relationship to be developed. The apostolic prophetic heart of God was sent to, and must restore grace. The apostle Paul dealt with this issue before the Galatians. In Galatians 3:1 he say's *"who has bewitched you"*

Ephesians 2:8 *"For by grace you have been saved through faith, and that not of yourselves; it is the gift of God,"*

Galatians 3:26 *"For you are all Son's of God through faith in Christ Jesus."*

Apostle Paul addresses the issue of the Galatians having started out in the spirit by faith, and then being dragged back into the flesh, and trying to please and live in relationship with God and one another, through struggling and striving to keep the laws of Moses through circumcision and sabbath keeping etc.

In Galatians 3:1 apostle Paul says, *"O foolish Galatians! Who has **bewitched you** that **you** should not obey the truth, before whose eyes Jesus Christ was clearly portrayed among **you** as crucified?"*

Mosaic-law-centred preaching and teaching is what many have run with for so long, but it doesn't produce the righteousness of God in the sons and daughters of God. It actually disempowers change and growth rather than facilitating and empowering transformation!

Much of what we have done has been behaviourally and psychologically focussed rather than *dying to self* and being washed by the word of God, and *Spiritually renewed and sanctified* by the working of the Holy Spirit. A cross-less, flesh motivated change that produces legalistic joyless servants, like the older son that remained in the house. Rather than a Joyful, thankful, Spirit-filled son or daughter of God that came to his senses in the pig pen as a prodigal and returned home as a true son to his father.

A negative behavioural focus, lends itself to establishing a repeat cycle of guilt, shame and failure over and over again. It is effective in convicting the prodigal sons and daughters of their sins, as the law was designed to do, but not effective in bringing the necessary change of heart for transformation, that leads to restoration!

Romans 7:7-12 *"[7]What shall we say then? Is the law sin? Certainly not! On the contrary, I would not have known sin except through the law. For I would not have known covetousness unless the law had said, "You shall not covet."[8]But sin, taking opportunity by the commandment, produced in me all manner of evil desire. For apart from the law sin was dead. [9]I was alive once without the law, but when the commandment came, sin revived and I died. [10]And the commandment, which was to bring life, I found to bring death. [11]For sin, taking occasion by the commandment, deceived me, and by it killed me. [12]Therefore the law is holy, and the commandment holy and just and good."*

Romans 7:19-20. *"For the good that I will to do, I do not do; but the evil I will not to do, that I practice. [20]Now if I do what I will not to do, it is no longer I who do it, but sin that dwells in me."*

Mosaic-law-centred preaching, teaching and spiritual parenting leaves the potential son or daughter of God with no real redemptive way back. They would not find their way to a real spiritual father or mother through this avenue without divine intervention.

But the apostolic prophetic heart of God in the apostle and prophet, through grace, will identify the God given potential in the son or daughter of God and help them to find their true identity in Christ

Galatians 3: 2 shows us that we can be-

Gal.3: 2b Sons of faith (Abraham and Grace) leading to promise and inheritance

OR

Gal.3: 2a Sons of the law (Moses and Works) which leads to living under the curse of the law, rules and regulations and never pleasing God.

Galatians 3:13 tells us *"Christ has redeemed us from the curse of the law, having become a curse for us (for it is written "cursed is everyone who is hanged on a tree")."*

Romans 8: 2 tells us that *"For the law of the Spirit of life in Christ Jesus has made me free from the law of sin and death".*

Grace makes way for the law of the Spirit of life in Christ Jesus. The sons of God are led by the Spirit of God. (Rom. 8:14)

Paul understood the law of liberty and grace as an apostle. 1 Corinthians 6: 12 says *"All things are lawful for me, but all things are not helpful. All things are lawful for me, but I will not be brought under the power of any."*

Fathers exercise grace and sons are produced by grace. They understand that the Lord is the Spirit and where the Spirit of the Lord is there is liberty and there is life (2 Corinthians 3:17).

Grace must be restored. Pharisees or legalists don't produce sons, but fathers do. Blind leaders of the blind don't produce sons. Pharisees, legalists and blind Leaders of the blind tend to produce slaves. They become servants and slaves to a man rather than sons and daughters that are connected to their Heavenly Father.

Ultimately, what is on the inside of you (in your heart and in your spirit); is potentially what you are able to reproduce. This highlights the seed to tree principle. You plant the seed, water it, cultivate it and watch it grow into a fruit-bearing tree. The seed takes root and produces fruit. Jesus said that we would know a tree by its fruit. So it is with a Father's heart. It can be known by his sons.

Ephesians 2:4-8 *"But God, who is rich in mercy, because of His great love with which He loved us, ⁵even when we were dead in trespasses, made us alive together with Christ (by grace you have been saved), ⁶and raised us up together, and made us sit together in the heavenly places in Christ Jesus, ⁷that in the ages to come He might show the exceeding riches of His grace in His kindness toward us in Christ Jesus. ⁸For by grace you have been saved through faith, and that not of yourselves; it is the gift of God, ⁹not of works, lest anyone should boast. ¹⁰For we are His workmanship, created in Christ Jesus for good works, which God prepared beforehand that we should walk in them."*

Grace helps the son or daughter find the path that the Lord has prepared for them to walk on. It helps them find there God given destiny and purpose in this life! Let us pray that many sons and daughters of God find the grace they need! We pray they connect with the right spiritual fathers and mothers that can be good role models for unity of the faith and unity of the Spirit. Amen!

****
Ephesians 4:1-6

"I, therefore, the prisoner of the Lord, beseech you to walk worthy of the calling with which you were called, ²with all lowliness and gentleness, with long-suffering, bearing with one another in love, ³endeavouring to keep the unity of the Spirit in the bond of peace. ⁴**There is one body and one Spirit, just as you were called in one hope of your calling;** *⁵one Lord, one faith, one baptism; ⁶one God and Father of all, who is above all, and through all, and in you all."*

****

CHAPTER TWELVE

Restoration of the Soul!

Mark 12:30 *"And you shall love the Lord your God with all your heart, with all your soul, with all your mind, and with all your strength.' This is the first commandment."*

Jesus instructs us to love the Lord our God with all our heart, **with all our soul**, with all our mind and with all our strength! This of course is difficult to do, when a person's soul is broken and needs fixing! A right and proper relationship with God is where it begins to take place

It is the restoration of the Soul; that the Spirit of God works towards, in those that are being fashioned and shaped as his sons and daughters. The restoration of the soul is where it starts after being *born again*. When I speak of soul, I am speaking of the collective of mind, will and emotions. Being transformed by the renewing of the mind (Romans 12:1-2), healing of the emotions & surrender of the will to God, as part of the restoration of the soul.

Psalm 23:3 say's *He restores my soul* this Psalm illustrates for us the need to allow God to be our Shepherd; and lead us to the place of *green pastures* and *still waters*. This means we must become as *sheep* and not remain as *goats*.

This means our soul is quieted with-in us as it says in Psalm 131:2. God our Heavenly Father and Shepherd, can strengthen, heal and make us whole. Ultimately, our soul will only find its rest and wholeness in God.

Psalm 23 *"The Lord is my shepherd; I shall not want. ²He makes me to lie down in green pastures; He leads me beside the still waters. ³He restores my soul; He leads me in the paths of righteousness for His name's sake.⁴ Yea, though I walk through the valley of the shadow of death, I will fear no evil; for You are with me; Your rod and Your staff, they comfort me. ⁵You prepare a table before me in the presence of my enemies; You anoint my head with oil; My cup runs over. ⁶Surely goodness and mercy shall follow me all the days of my life; and I will dwell in the house of the Lord forever."*

This means the *rod of correction* for discipline will be used at certain times and at other times the *staff of guidance* will be used. The scripture speaks of both as bringing *comfort*.

Hebrews 12:3-11 *"⁷if you endure chastening, God deals with you as with sons; for what son is there whom a father does not chasten? ⁸But if you are without chastening of which all have become partakers, then you are illegitimate and not sons."*

⁹ᵇ...Shall we not much more readily be in subjection to the Father(God)of spirits and live?"

A Principle to live by: Co-operation*(with the Holy Spirit)* and Subjection *(to the Father)* leads to Restoration.

Co-operation with the Spirit of God (Spirit of Adoption, Spirit of Sonship) leads to God's restoration of an individual's soul. It's about dealing with the sin problem and restoring the image of man back to the image of God through Jesus Christ.

Ephesians 4:11-15 tells us that *"¹¹And He Himself, gave some to be apostles, some prophets, some evangelists, and some pastors and teachers, ¹²for the **equipping** of the saints for the **work of ministry**, for the **edifying** of the body of Christ; ¹³till we all come to **unity** of the faith and of the **knowledge** of the Son of God, to a **perfect man**, to the measure of the stature of the **fullness** of Christ ¹⁴ that we should **no longer be children**, tossed to and fro and carried about with every wind of doctrine, by the trickery of men, in the cunning craftiness of deceitful plotting, "¹⁵......may **grow up** in all things into Him......"*

The ascension gifts are given to bring restoration, maturity, growth. A mature family is what God wants. A fully grown *corporate son* (the Church) is a part of the apostolic prophetic heart's desire.

The restoration of man's soul is where it begins. Mind, will and emotions are all part of the whole or total person. We must bring restoration to the *whole* not just the *part*. The whole church corporately, as well as the whole person individually.

Father God is working through true fathers and mothers to restore the soul. If your soul needs restoring then ask God to lead you into relationship with a true father or mother in the faith.

3 John 2 say's *"Beloved I pray that you may prosper in all things and be in health, just as your soul prospers."*

The *whole* as well as the *part* must be restored. Just sticking band-aids and only dealing with symptoms is not sufficient for restoration of the soul. The prospering of the soul is a key to every thing else being restored. (see latter pages in this book for relevant diagram)

Ezekiel 37:1-14 presents to us a picture of bringing together the parts to make the whole. Bringing together dead dry bones, scattered in no particular order. No life, just death. Bones brought back together to form multiple complete skeletons with flesh being placed back on the bones and then God breathing His Spirit back into them.

"¹The hand of the Lord came upon me and brought me out in the Spirit of the Lord, and set me down in the midst of the valley; and it was full of bones. ²Then He caused me to pass by them all around, and behold, there were very many in the open valley; and indeed they were very dry."

Apostles and prophets in particular are called and gifted to bring together the parts, the structure, the frame, the foundation of *the house, the building, the temple, the family, the body.* Speaking to the bones, prophesying to the bones, just as prophet Ezekiel did.

"⁴Again He said to me, "Prophesy to these bones, and say to them, 'O dry bones, hear the word of the Lord!" ⁷So I prophesied as I was commanded; and as I prophesied, there was a noise, and suddenly a rattling; and the bones came together, bone to bone. ⁸Indeed, as I looked, the sinews and the flesh came upon them, and the skin covered them over; but there was no breath in them."

Bones speak of foundation and structure. Sometimes bones need to be broken and reset, re-aligned, re-fashioned, refitted.

Psalm 34: 20 *"He guards all his bones; Not one of them is broken"* It is worth noting that none of Jesus bones were broken in the customary manner of crucifixion on the cross (John 19:36). This was normally done to complete the death cycle. Why? Because, He was and is the perfect, mature Son of God. Jesus was totally and completely surrendered to His Father, even to the point of death.

The breaking of bones is sometimes necessary when they are not correctly aligned. With-in bones there is marrow and with-in the marrow; blood is produced. Scripture says the life is in the blood (Leviticus 17:11). No blood supply, then no life, no life then you end up with dead dry bones.

Rightly Joined Rightly Connected!

Being Rightly Joined and Rightly Connected is necessary for the life of God's spirit to flow and for restoration to take place.

The apostolic prophetic heart facilitates being rightly joined and rightly connected. It makes way for the breath of God to flow into the bones (structure) putting sinew and flesh on the bones and body by decreeing and declaring the living word. These are the parenting and foundation laying gifts and ministries that Jesus gave to His family, His Church.

1 Peter 2:5a *"You also as living stones are being built up a spiritual house..."*

Haggai 2:9 *"The glory of this latter temple (house) shall be greater than the former,' says the lord of hosts. 'And in this place I will give peace,' says the Lord of hosts."*

The sons and daughters of God must have restored souls to stand firm and strong! Many are suffering from what I like to call *connection deprivation or* a bad connection.

Hebrews 10:24-26 says *"24 And let us consider one another in order to stir up love and good works, 25 not forsaking the assembling of ourselves together, as is the manner of some, but exhorting one another, and so much the more as you see the Day approaching."*

Many forsake gathering face to face, and as a result miss out on the stirring up of the Spirit that happens when the sons and daughters of God gather together in fellowship. Being knit together, joined together in the Spirit requires a face to face, heart to heart connection!

In relation to the connection of believers and fellowship of the Holy Spirit it says in 2 Corinthians 13:14 *"The grace of the Lord Jesus Christ, and the love of God, and* **the communion (fellowship) of the Holy Spirit** *be with you all. Amen"* Much nourishment and edification comes this way.

Concerning our connection with one another in Christ, it says in Ephesians 4:16 ..."*from whom the whole body, joined and knit together by what every joint supplies, according to the effective working by which every part does its share, causes growth of the body for the edifying of itself in love.*" "...*by what every joint supplies...*" is the Christ centred connection between each of the members that contributes to the whole. The soul needs to be in the restoration process to contribute to this out-working in *the body* between the sons and daughters of God.

To be a *living stone* we must be *connected* with not only Christ, but with the body of Christ! The picture of the *vine and the branches* in John 15:1-5 highlights this truth perfectly.

The glory of the *latter house* will be seen, when the sons and daughters of God have a lively connection with Christ and with one another. The restoration of the soul will increasingly make way for this to happen, as the *'Ruach HaKodesh'* (the breath of God) is able to quicken the sons and daughters of God without any form of hindrance or obstruction.

****
Luke 1:46-47
"*[46] And Mary said:* **my soul magnifies the Lord,**
[47] And my spirit rejoiced in God my Saviour"
****

CHAPTER THIRTEEN

Restoring the Soul and Diagram!

Restoring the soul of human beings, has always been central to God's heart and redemptive plan. In using the term soul, I am referring to the mind, will and emotions of a human being!

Man as a three part being is made up of: 1. *Body,* 2. *Soul, and* 3. *Spirit*. This is what theologians refer to as being a *tripartite* being! Then within the *soul* there is *mind, will* and *emotions*.

There is also a couple of other terms that theologians use in reference to man's anthropological make up as follows: 1. Trichotomy & 2. Dichotomy.

Those who believe that human beings are a trichotomy, believe that they are made up of body, soul and spirit, with the soul and spirit existing as separate components in mans make up.

1 Thessalonians 5:23 says *"Now may the God of peace Himself sanctify you completely, and may your whole **spirit, soul and body** be preserved blameless at the coming of our Lord Jesus Christ."*

Those who believe that human beings are a dichotomy also believe that we are made up of body, soul and spirit, but hold to the idea that the soul and spirit do not exist separately; but rather as joined together and inseparable.

As it says in Hebrews 4:12, It is the word of God only, that can *separate soul* and *spirit, bone* and *marrow, thought* and *intent*. Human wisdom and reasoning cannot separate soul and spirit.

"For the word of God is living and powerful, and sharper than any two-edged sword, piercing even to the division of soul and spirit, and of joints and marrow, and is a discerner of the thoughts and intents of the heart."

The difference between the two views revolves around the idea of the soul and spirit either being separable or inseparable. These ideas at their root are heavily influenced by Hellenistic or Greek thought and culture, as much of the New Testament was originally written in the common man's (koine') Greek of the day!

If we look at the original Hebrew language and mind set associated with the Old Testament, we discover that human beings are referred to in a way that suggests they are made up of the *material* and *immaterial*. The *physical* and the *spiritual*. The body being associated with the physical and the *heart, mind, thoughts, emotions* being associated with the spiritual.

Matthew 11:29 says *"Take My yoke upon **you** and learn from Me, for I am gentle and lowly in heart, and **you will find rest for your souls.**"*

Everything that Jesus was sent by the Father to do in His earthly ministry, revolved around the redeeming, washing and cleansing of man's soul. Hence the need for forgiveness and healing the brokenhearted! *Rest* comes to the soul of those who receive his forgiveness and healing. Restoration of the soul is the end result, for those who learn of his ways and receive of His mercy and truth.

The true apostolic prophetic heart of God in those He raises to be spiritual fathers and mothers, will always seek to connect the spiritual son or daughter to the *Great Shepherd*, that their soul might be restored.

In Psalm 23 as follows, we see depicted the care of a watchful, protective shepherd, just like a loving father, who takes care of his son or daughter. Bringing healing, refreshing and restoration. Taking care of, and providing for every need. Offering safety, protection and victory over enemies

"¹ The Lord is my shepherd; I shall not want. ²He makes me to lie down in green pastures;
*He leads me beside the still waters. ³**He restores my soul;** He leads me in the paths of righteousness for His name's sake. ⁴Yea, though I walk through the valley of the shadow of death, I will fear no evil;*

For You are with me; Your rod and Your staff, they comfort me. ⁵You prepare a table before me in the presence of my enemies; You anoint my head with oil; My cup runs over.
⁶Surely goodness and mercy shall follow me All the days of my life; And I will dwell in the house of the Lord forever."

Sin leads to brokenness and woundedness of the soul. For many of us, our mind, will and emotions have become like a city described in ancient times, as having *broken down walls* or no walls.

In ancient times; cities had walls built around them; to protect against the attacks of hostile parties and antagonistic neighbouring areas, cities and towns.

Nehemiah 2:11-17 is a good example of this. Nehemiah went and viewed the state of Jerusalem and its broken down walls. Father God had placed it in Nehemiah's heart to rebuild those walls.

For many, their Soul (mind, will and emotions) has become just like a city with no walls, or broken down walls. Open to every onslaught of the enemy (Satan).

Every fiery dart, every temptation that comes along they cannot withstand or gain victory over. Their soul is weak and sick. No strength, no health, just pain and brokenness.

Just like the enemies of God against Nehemiah and God's people rebuilding the Jerusalem walls. They were mocked, jeered, discouraged, tormented, intimidated and attacked. (See Nehemiah 2: 19, 4:1,3, 6:9)

Everything in our relationship with God is filtered through our soul. If God wants to shine out of us from within the place of our spirit, then the light of His Spirit must pass through our soul. If our soul is in need of restoration, then only pain and sorrow will be seen. A principle truth that relates to this can be found in

Matthew 6:22-23 as follows: *"²²The lamp of the body is the eyes. If therefore your eye is good, your whole body will be full of light. ²³But if your eye is bad, your whole body will be full of darkness. If therefore the light that is in you is darkness, how great is that darkness"*

A wounded soul is often either numbed or over sensitized by pain and in darkness, but a healthy soul is like a clean piece of glass, that light can freely pass through!

The old cliche holds true, *hurt people, hurt people.* Wounded people, wound people. Why? Because their soul needs restoring.

The life of God that should flow out of our spirit where we commune with Him, is what should shine forth. It must all filter through the realm of mind, will and emotions. Hence the need for a renewed mind, a surrendered will, and emotions that are subject to the *Word of God* and the *Spirit of God*.

God desires the restoration of our soul. Just like the decision Nehemiah made to rebuild the walls, so too must we make the decision to work in co-operation with God the Father's Spirit for the restoration of our soul.

Psalm 23:3 say's "*He restores my soul*" but it requires that we allow him to lead us beside still waters and make us to "*lie down in green pastures*" (verse 2). Our soul needs food, the kind of food that only our Shepherd can lead us to, in His green pastures.

Jesus tells us in John 7: 38 that he that believes (trusts) in Me, out of his belly (heart, ***soul***), will flow rivers of living water.

If our soul needs restoration then we must allow him to lead us beside *"still waters"*. Jesus is the Father's *still waters*. Still waters are calm waters. They are not shallow rapids. Still waters are usually wide and deep. They are quiet. They are not noisy with a lot of froth and bubble.

If we learn to come to the Father's *still waters* then we will as a result, see a river flow out of us, that will affect others around us with true spiritual life.

Jesus was never in a hurry. He saw what the Father showed Him in the spirit realm and then acted. He heard what the Father said to Him and spoke accordingly. In the place of our soul being restored is where we learn to do the same.

Matthew 4:4 tells us that our soul must feed on the word of God. *"But He answered and said, "It is written, 'Man shall not live by bread alone, but by every word that proceeds from the mouth of God.'"*

Faith comes by hearing, and hearing by the word of God (Rom.10: 17). So even in the realm of our five senses i.e. our sense of taste, touch, smell, seeing and hearing, we must learn to listen and discern the right things.

Our five senses are *gateways* to either our *spirit* or our *soul*. Depending on *who* or *what* we are yielded to, will determine *how* we are led and who or what we come in contact with.

Our spirit, which is where we commune with God, must be allowed to rule over our soul and body. The scripture in Galatians 5:16 calls it walking in the Spirit. *"I say then: Walk in the Spirit, and you shall not fulfill the lust of the flesh."*

Faith rather than our five senses, must come into operation as we trust God, in the application of His word. Our five senses at times do not always communicate to us truth. The scripture tells us in Hebrews 11:1 that faith is being sure of what we hope for; and certain of what we do not see.

The apostle John in 3 John verse 2 prays a very important and life changing prayer. It says *"Beloved I pray that you may prosper in all things and be in health, just as your soul prospers."*

This prayer of John's shows the heart of a true spiritual father and clearly teaches us that the prospering, restoring of our soul is the key to restoration happening in every area of our lives. It is God's intention that we should truly be blessed and prospering physically, spiritually, emotionally, mentally, relationally etc., as sons and daughters of God.

Psalm 100:4 Says that we should *"Enter into His gates with thanksgiving, And into His courts with praise. Be thankful to Him, and bless His name."* This scripture is based on the basic pattern of the Old Testament tabernacle.

We can draw a parallel between the Old Testament tabernacle and the body, soul and spirit of man, along with his five senses.

There is a diagram that follows further on in this chapter, to help understand the parallel/comparison being made.

Let me make the comparison as follows:

1. The Five SENSES equate to the *gates* in which we are to enter; with *"thanksgiving"*.

We enter his *Gates* = FIVE SENSES with *Thanksgiving*.

Our 5 Senses: Hearing, Seeing, Smell, Taste, Touch) If we allow it, our Five senses can either *strengthen* or *undermine* our faith and trust in God!

Our five senses have a corresponding spiritual blue print which must connect with our Spirit once we are *born again*. They should be a gateway seen in spiritual ears, eyes, smell, taste & touch.

For example, there are times when one can smell or taste *pride*, or taste and feel the *presence* of the Lord. When the spirit of God is made manifest through the anointing at work, we can have many sensory responses and reactions that reveal this spiritual blue print, that connects the natural with the spiritual. People operating in occult practices and witchcraft know and understand such things.

I have placed the following scriptures here as an attempt to show that we can have spiritual senses functioning, that correlate with our natural senses as we endeavour to walk with the Lord.

HEARING- Romans 10:17 *"So then faith comes by **hearing**, and hearing by the word of God."* This tells us our sense of hearing corresponds to hearing the word of God, where faith must be encouraged and therefore a response to God, which is based on His unchanging word.

Matthew 23:13 "*But he who received seed on the good ground is he who **bears** the word and understands it, who indeed bears fruit and produces: some a hundredfold, some sixty, some thirty.*"

Revelation 2:7 "*He who has an **ear**, let him **hear** what the Spirit says to the churches.*" (see also Rev. 2:11, 17, 29, Rev 3:6,13,22)

Note: It is worth noting as a general rule, that the last of the five senses a person loses before departing their physical body, is their sense of hearing!

SEEING- Ephesians 1:18 "*the **eyes of your understanding** being enlightened; that you may know what is the hope of His calling, what are the riches of the glory of His inheritance in the saints,*"

SMELL- 2 Corinthians 2:15-16 "*For we are to God the **fragrance** of Christ among those who are being saved and among those who are perishing. ¹⁶ To the one we are the aroma of death leading to death, and to the other the aroma of life leading to life. And who is sufficient for these things?*"

TASTE- Psalm 34:8 "*Oh, taste and see that the Lord is good; blessed is the man who trusts in him!*"

TOUCH- Mark 5:31 "*But His disciples said to Him, "You see the multitude thronging You, and You say, 'Who **touched** Me?*"

2. **The BODY** equates to the *outer court* in which we are to enter; with *"praise"*.

We enter his *Courts/Outer Court* = BODY with Praise

3. The SOUL equates to the *inner court* in which we are to enter; also with *"praise"*.

We enter his *Courts/Inner Court* = SOUL *(Mind, Will & Emotions)* with Praise.

4. The SPIRIT equates to the *holy of holies* in which we are to enter into, in *"worship"* (*spirit & truth* John 4: 23 - 24) This is the place in which Jesus enters when we receive him as Saviour.

We enter the *Holy of Holies* = SPIRIT with *Worship (in Spirit & Truth).*

Jesus made a way for us to enter the Holy of Holies through His blood that was shed and offered for our sin. Scripture tells us that He is our *High Priest* as well as being the *Sacrifice*. He has entered the Holy of Holies and made a way for us to enter. (Hebrews 2: 10,17, 4: 14-16, 5: 11.)

Once a year in the Old Testament Tabernacle; the High Priest would enter the Holy of Holies and offer the blood of a sacrificed animal on the mercy seat, between the wings of the cherubim that sat over the ark of the covenant. This was for the atonement of the people's sins.

Hebrews 9:7 says *"But into the second part the high priest went alone once a year, not without blood, which he offered for himself and for the people's sins committed in ignorance"*

In 1 Corinthians 6:18-20 we are told to *"[18]Flee sexual immorality. Every sin that a man does is outside the body, but he who commits sexual immorality sins against his own body. [19]Or do you not know that your body is the temple of the Holy Spirit who is in you, whom you have from God, and you are not your own? [20]For you were bought at a price; therefore glorify God in your body and in your spirit, which are God's.*

This scripture shows us that as human beings, we can be corrupted by sin and immorality. We need to be reminded that we are now the temple of God. We are no longer our own, We belong to God. We have been bought at a price. That is the blood of Christ. Therefore we are to glorify God in body, soul and spirit.

The soul is that part of man, that the Spirit of God will constantly work towards restoring, by appropriating the sacrifice of Christ and His healing restoring power.

Many times the body manifests the fruits of an unhealthy soul. Doctors call it psychosomatic illness. Sickness in the body that has a direct connection with what is happening in the soul. The body manifests the soul's condition.

In the Gospel of John 5:1-15 Jesus healed a man, sick with an infirmity for 38 yrs, laying on a mat at the pool of Bethesda waiting for a miracle. He told him to *go and sin no more* after he was healed. The Soul that is sick, is bound by sin and as a result, they suffer in their physical body, whether as a result of direct or indirect sin.

The man at the pool of Bethesda had a problem that started with his soul and manifested in his body. The apostle John prayed that we would prosper in all things and be in health; even as our soul prospers (3 John verse 2). If there is no healing or restoration in the soul, then there can be no lasting or maintained physical healing! The same can be said for the person who is delivered from a demon/evil spirit/unclean spirit, but has not received any healing or restoration in their soul. Deliverance will not be maintained without it.

1 Thessalonians 5:23 says "Now *may the God of peace Himself sanctify you completely, and may your whole spirit, soul and body be preserved blameless at the coming of our Lord Jesus Christ.*"

The whole person is seen here in this verse of scripture from 1 Thessalonians chapter 5, where body, soul and spirit is acknowledged. God is interested in the whole person but restoration of the soul is of primary importance.

Human beings have now become temples of the living God, *temples of the Holy Spirit*, in which His work of restoration can take place beginning in the the human soul.

1 Corinthians 6:19 *"Or do you not know that your body is the temple of the Holy Spirit who is in you, whom you have from God......?"*

The Christian who has truly put their faith, their trust in Jesus and His finished work on the cross at Calvary, who is truly born of the Spirit of God, has now become the *'temple of God'*, the *'temple of the Holy Spirit'*

In 1 Corinthians 3:16-17 it says, *"^{16} Do you not know that you are the temple of God and that the Spirit of God dwells in you? ^{17} If anyone defiles the temple of God, God will destroy him.* **For the temple of God is holy, which temple you are.**

Defilement of the temple is where the ***sanctification and restoration*** of its equivalent, that is the soul, must first begin to take place.

Sons and daughters of God must connect with God in their spirit and be led by the Spirit of God. Romans 8:14 says *"For as many as are led by the Spirit of God, these are sons of God."*

If we are purely sensory in our responses, that is making decisions and acting based on our five senses, without God's leading through his word and His Spirit, then our senses will either undermine or deceive us.

The following diagram is a simplified visual comparison between the Old Testament temple/tabernacle (Exodus 25:1-40:38, 2 Chronicles Ch's 3-6) and the tripartite structure of a human being as the temple of the Holy Spirit.

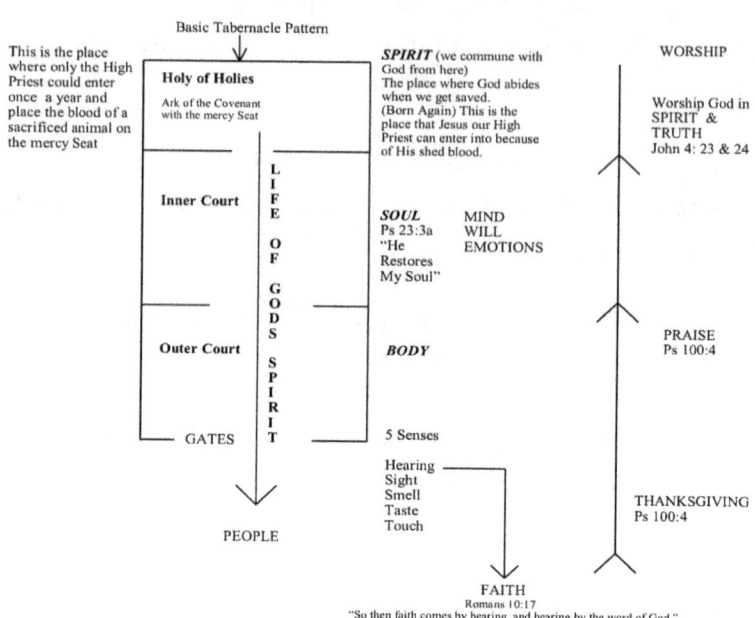

O.T. Temples comparison with the Tripartite make up of a Human Being
Credit: Patrick M. O'Neal(2006)

God is Spirit. He is to be worshiped in Spirit & Truth... John 4:23-24 says,

"23 But the hour is coming, and now is, when the true worshipers will worship the Father in spirit and truth; for the Father is seeking such to worship Him. 24 God is Spirit, and those who worship Him must worship in spirit and truth."

We are sanctified in Spirit, Soul & Body... 1 Thessalonians 5:23 says,

"Now may the God of peace Himself sanctify you completely; and may your whole spirit, soul, and body be preserved blameless at the coming of our Lord Jesus Christ."

Prosperity and Blessing must begin in the Soul ... 3 John verse 2 says,

"Beloved I pray that you may prosper in all things and be in health, just as your soul prospers" Our Soul's prosperity / sanctification/ restoration/ healing is foundational to our whole *person* being restored!

If we are not being transformed by the renewing of our mind through the word of God, then our soul is not being restored. Romans 12:1-2 says,

"I beseech you therefore, brethren, by the mercies of God, that you present your bodies a living sacrifice, holy, acceptable to God, which is your reasonable service. ²And do not be conformed to this world, but be transformed by the renewing of your mind, that you may prove what is that good and acceptable and perfect will of God."

This scripture dispels the myth that our body doesn't matter. That we can do with it whatever we like, in how we live. The fact is, our body, soul and spirit all belong to God! The soul's restoration requires the mind to be renewed and the body to be surrendered to God for His perfect will to be done.

Emotions are very subjective and changeable. If we just allow emotions to determine our choices and actions, then there is a good chance that we are being led away from God into paths of destruction. Which means our soul is not in restoration mode.

If our *will* is not *surrendered* to God as the leader and Lord of our life, then our soul will not find its ultimate restoration. Restoration of the soul leads to the *whole* person being restored. Total restoration means total healing. The *whole* person is to be redeemed, reconciled, revived and restored.

May many restored souls find their true identity as sons and daughters in Him! Let us pray that many souls are restored as sons and daughters of the most High God through the blood of Jesus!

Let us pray that the souls of the sons and daughters of God are set alight with the fire of the Holy Spirit. Amen!   Let me close this chapter with the following passage...

***

Psalm 103:1-4
"Bless the Lord, O my soul;
and all that is within me,
bless His holy name!
²Bless the Lord, O my soul,
and forget not all His benefits:
³Who forgives all your iniquities,
Who heals all your diseases,
⁴Who redeems your life from destruction,
Who crowns you with loving kindness
and tender mercies"

***

CHAPTER FOURTEEN

Restoration of All Things List & Flow Chart!

The apostolic prophetic heart of God is a primary part of a hastening towards perfection, maturity and purity in the sons and daughters of God (among other things), before the Son of God can be sent at His second coming!
Following is a list and a flow-chart diagram; of important *Kingdom business* that the Spirit of God is involved in hastening towards restoring *in* and *through* the apostolic prophetic heart, in His Church, on the earth, according to the divine pattern of fatherhood and sonship!

*Ascension Gift Ministries (Five-Fold) Apostles, Prophets, Evangelists, Pastors and Teachers. Ephesians. 4:11-16, 1 Corinthians 12:5.

*The Fathers. This in particular, applies to the apostles and prophets. Malachi 4:6, 1 Cor. 4:15, 2 Kings 2:12

*Fatherhood. Luke 15:11-22, Eph. 3: 5, 1 Corinthians.4: 15-16, 1 Corinthians.11: 1.

*Sonship. Romans 8: 14-17, Ephesians 1:5, Galatians 4:6, 1 John 3:1.

The Family of God. Ephesians 3: 9, 10, 15, Ephesians 2:19, 1 John 3:1-2, Romans 8:16-17.

Relationship, The Church. John 15: 1-5. 1 Timothy 3:15, Matthew 16:18-20, John 13:34, 1 Corinthians 12:13.

Foundations. Hebrews 12:12-13, 28-29, Ephesians 2:20, 1 Corinthians 3: 9-10, Isaiah 58:12, Ezekiel 37:1-10.

Covenant. Ezekiel16: 60, Hebrews 13:20.

Grace. Galatians 3:1-2, Ephesians 2:8.

Faith. Hebrews 11:1, Galatians 3:8, Romans 4:12, Genesis 22:1.

Unity. Ephesians 4:1-6, Psalm 133.

Gifts and Callings. Romans 11:29, Romans 12:6, 1 Peter 4:10, Romans 12:4, 1 Timothy 4:14, Proverbs 18:16, 1 Corinthians 12:4, 1 Corinthians 7:7, 1 Cor.14:1

Inheritance. Ezekiel 46: 16-18, Romans 8: 17.

Revelation of Jesus. Isaiah 6:1, Colossians 2:4-10, John 14:8-10, Rev. 1:9-16, Acts 26:9-20, Philippians 3:3-14, Acts 7:55.

The Soul. 3 John 2, Psalm 23:3, 1 Thessalonians 5:23, Luke 1:46.

The restoration of all things according to God's divine order and plan, is necessary before Christ can return. It is, as spoken by all the holy prophets that have gone before at God's command. As it says in Proverbs 24:3-4 *"³Through wisdom a house is built, and by understanding it is established; ⁴by knowledge the rooms are filled with all precious and pleasant riches."* The apostolic prophetic heart builds according to God the Fathers' blue print. They do it His way, according to His pattern, in His time. The Father's purpose and plan is number one, to every true apostle and prophet, just as it was to King David and His son Solomon, in the building of the early O.T. Temple (1 Chronicle 28).

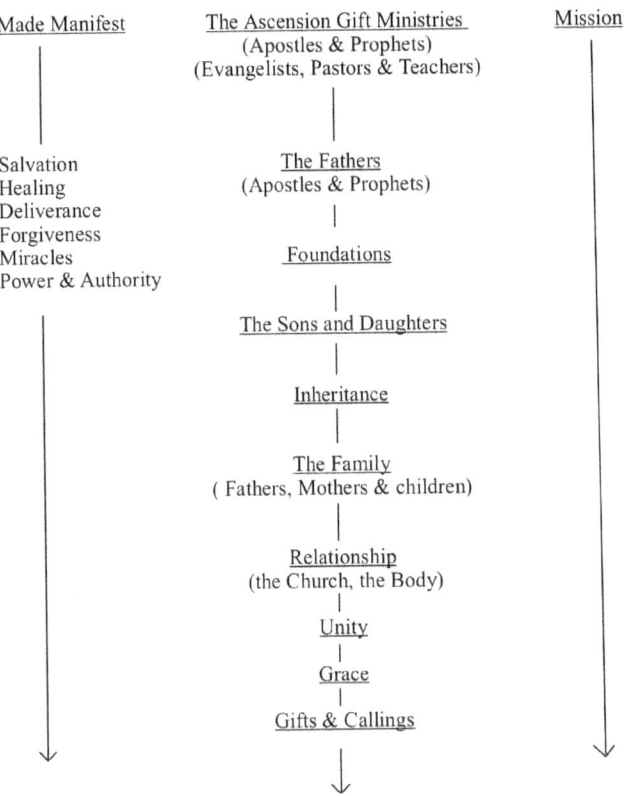

Flow Chart
Credit: Patrick M. O'Neal (2006)

The *latter-day* divine purpose and plan (which part of it's process can be seen in the proceeding flow-chart diagram) within the heart of God our *Father*, our *Creator*, has always been *a man* that would be His son. A man, a woman that walks with God. Created according to His order, and bearing His own image.

But not just one son, but rather many sons bearing His image. The same image that Adam was bearing before the fall in the garden of Eden. An unbroken, restored image, that would be found in *many sons* that would reflect His character, His nature, His heart, His calling, His purpose, His gifts, His redemptive love.

Many sons, that would as a group, become a community, *a corporate body*. His bride, His *holy ones* that would remain immovable, uncompromising, pure, relational, organic. Trusting Him no matter what comes their way on the earth, whether principality, personality or problem.

A corporate body that the Father could look upon and see as a *mature corporate son*. A corporate son that looks just like Jesus. A corporate son that manifests the work of restoration, accomplished by the Life changing work of His only begotten Son Jesus Christ, on the cross at the Calvary

Sons are daughters that are as a people, that arise and shine with His glory. Ready to serve Him and His eternal purpose. Ready to lay down their lives for Him, no matter what persecution or trials they face. Ready to welcome Him and receive Him, at His return!

The sons and daughters of God are the *living stones*. They are the Family of God in heaven and earth. A living breathing temple filled with the Spirit of God. 1 Peter 2:4-5 *"Coming to Him as to a living stone, rejected indeed by men, but chosen by God and precious, ⁵you also, as living stones, are being built up a spiritual house, a holy priest-hood, to offer up spiritual sacrifices acceptable to God through Jesus Christ."*

The revealed sons and daughters of God will make up the temple of the latter days, the *spiritual house* that is more glorious than the former temple ever was!

The apostolic prophetic heart of God is truly the heart of the Father, given to those called to the gifting of apostle and prophet in these last days! The family of God is what they have a real concern for.

Ephesians 3:1-21 *"14For this reason I bow my knee to the Father of our Lord Jesus Christ, 15from whom the **whole family in heaven and earth** is named."*

They have a burden for the Church, the members of God's family, those that are lost, those that are back-slidden. Those that need to shift from prodigal to true son or daughter! They understand that God our Father gave His only begotten Son to produce sons.

They believe and stand on the prophetic promise that, the glory of the latter house shall be greater than the former! Haggai 2: 9 *"For the glory of this latter temple shall be greater than the former.."*

The sons and daughters of God are the living stones, the *fiery* ones, *the light bearers* that the father is ultimately counting on to effect great change in the earth, as they walk in the Spirit with the fire of God burning in their hearts, preaching and demonstrating the message of the cross with signs and wonders following!

They are the *holy ones* that will bear His image and reflect His glory all over the earth. The dear ones that Christ shall return for, at his second coming. Christ in *you*, Christ in *me*, Christ in *us*, the hope of Glory!

Let us pray the apostles and prophets arise, and find their divinely appointed sphere. Their place and territory of influence in the earth, as true fathers and mothers to the sons and daughters assigned to them by the Father! Amen!

2 Corinthians 3:18

".....beholding as in a mirror the glory of the Lord, **are being transformed into the same image** *from glory to glory, just as by the Spirit of the Lord."*

CHAPTER FIFTEEN

Conclusion to the Apostolic Prophetic Heart of God!

It is my hope that you have benefited from this brief writing on *'The Apostolic Prophetic Heart of God"*. As with all things that God gives an understanding of, there is a progression and an unfolding. To whom much is given, much is required. The first shall be last and the last shall be first.

The greatest of all shall be the servant of all. Such is the nature of those He calls and sends. So shall it be for those who count the cost and answer the call. Let us become wise, humble and gracious in our serving. Let us serve as *Sons* and not as *Slaves,* willingly, purposefully and with a pure and sincere heart.

We know in part and we prophesy in part, but let us live up to the measure of truth and revelation that we have been given by our Heavenly Father. As apostle Paul says in Philippians 3:12-14 *"[12]Not that I have already attained, or am already perfected; but I press on, that I may lay hold of that for which Christ Jesus has also laid hold of me. [13]Brethren, I do not count myself to have apprehended; but one thing I do, forgetting* *those things which are behind and reaching forward to those things which are ahead, ^{14}I press toward the goal for the prize of the upward call of God in Christ Jesus."*

Every son and daughter of God should aim to grow and become fathers and mothers in the faith. In turn they should aim to restore all things back to God, even as their fathers and mothers in the faith have done. The washing, cleansing and redeeming power of Jesus blood still avails. The release of great faith and power still comes through the preaching of the gospel.

It is my hearts desire and prayer that you discover your place, level and function in Christ. That you live and serve accordingly as a son or daughter of God, and then eventually become a mature spiritual father or mother. That you would in turn be part of facilitating the bringing of many sons and daughters to Glory for God!

If you have been drawn by the Spirit to read this book, then chances are God is speaking to you about serving Him in an apostolic prophetic call. If you are hungry for more after reading this brief book then I would suggest that you are at the very least an apostle or prophet in the making. If you are going through a time of great and intense testing as you read this, then be encouraged, God is fashioning and preparing you.

If you are suffering great rejection and persecution, and none are standing with you, then also be encouraged. Great is your reward and great is the work Jesus has for you, that lays ahead.

If you are still not sure and don't understand what is happening in your life right now; then put your hand in His and simply trust him. Pray for divine appointments and divine connections and let Him work out His plan for you! He is getting things ready.

The bigger and greater the work He has for you; then the deeper the foundations must go, and the more highly refined the building materials must be. Remember gold, silver and precious stones remain, but hay, wood and stubble are consumed by fire! God doesn't build on sand, He builds on rock *'The Rock'* JESUS!

Colossians 1:2 *"To them God willed to make known what are the riches of the glory of this mystery among the Gentiles: which is Christ in you, the hope of glory."*

Remember it is Jesus and only Jesus, not Jesus plus what we think and what we think we can add. Let us be reminded of what Jesus says to the Laodiceans in the book of Revelation...

Revelation 3:18 *"[18] I counsel you to buy from Me gold refined in the fire, that you may be rich; and white garments, that you may be clothed, that the shame of your nakedness may not be revealed; and anoint your eyes with eye salve, that you may see. [19] As many as I love, I rebuke and chasten."*

Let us be ready to be made a son or daughter of the Most High God at what ever price He requires us to pay. The benefits are life changing and eternal. The fruit will remain.

As the scripture says in Isaiah 60:1 *"Arise, shine; for your light has come! And the glory of the Lord is risen upon you."* The glory of God will reveal the sons and daughters of God in this hour.

All of creation is in birth pains and waiting! Let us pray that this time and season is not delayed on God's prophetic time clock. Amen!

****

Romans 8:22-23

"²² *For we know that* **the whole creation groans and labors with birth pangs together until now.** ²³*Not only that, but we also who have the first fruits of the Spirit, even we ourselves groan within ourselves,* **eagerly waiting for the adoption, the redemption of our body.**"

****

CHAPTER SIXTEEN

Family History and Spiritual Heritage!

Ps Albert & Mr Mary Lowe, standing out the
front of 'Richmond Temple' in Richmond, Vic.
Australia in the Mid 1920's
Credit: Patrick M. O'Neal

Above is a photo of Patrick M. O'Neal's paternal great grandparents, Ps. Albert and Mrs Mary Lowe standing out the front of the old theatre, in Bridge Rd, Richmond, Victoria, Australia, which became the home of 'Richmond Temple'. The church was born out of the Sunshine Revival in the West of Melbourne, in the early to mid 1920's. It eventually became known as Richmond A.O.G. and the beginnings of the 'Assemblies of God', part of the early Pentecostal movement in Australia.

Ps Albert and Mrs Mary Lowe served as associates along side Ps C.L. Greenwood at 'Richmond Temple'. They were part of the original small group of people that had gathered regularly, week after week and prayed and sought God in a little scout hall in the suburb of Sunshine. God moved and poured out His Holy Spirit in revival. After many years, 'Richmond Temple' eventually relocated to a nearby warehouse, that was fitted out for the ever increasing congregation.

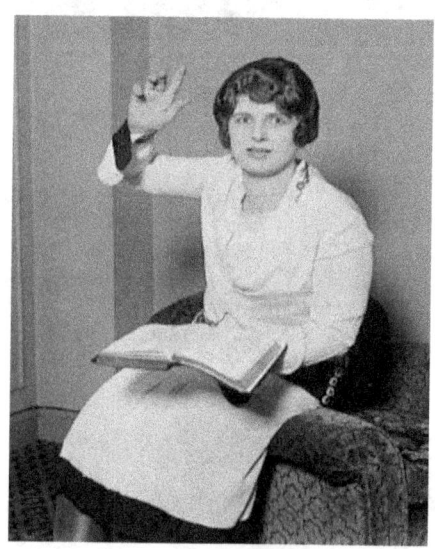

Aimee Semple-McPherson (1927)
Public Domain: Library of Congress USA

Aimee Semple-McPherson (9th October 1890 to 27th September 1944) a Canadian Pentecostal Evangelist and the founder of the Four Square Movement. Aimee came to Sydney and Melbourne, Australia in 1922. She founded the Four Square Church in 1923 in Los Angeles, USA.

The vision and name that she gave to the Four Square Church is based on the following four aspects of Christ: 1. *Saviour* 2. *Holy Spirit Baptiser* 3. *Healer* 4. *Soon* and *Coming King*.

Evangelist A.C. Valdez Snr. (1896 to 1981)
Public Domain: A.C.Valdez Project. acvaldez.org

Men such as Internationally recognised Latino Evangelist A.C (Adolph Clarence) Valdez Sr, (born 1896, died 1981) also came to Australia and New Zealand helping to establish the Pentecostal movement. He was also a witness of The Azusa Street Revival.

He held big tent revivals and evangelistic crusades. He pastored many churches of his own, but his heart was always in itinerant ministry!

He came to Australia for two yrs in the 1920's working with Southern Evangelical Mission and Sunshine Gospel Hall, which led to the beginning of the Pentecostal Movement in Australia

God's servant, Smith Wigglesworth, (a plumber who got so busy preaching he couldn't do plumbing anymore) was born in Menston, United Kingdom on the 10th June 1859 and died in Wakefield, United Kingdom on 12th March in 1947.

He first came to Melbourne, Australia on the 16th of February 1922 in answer to many prayers and the cries of God's people in Australia.

He conducted meetings at Good News Hall in Nth Melbourne and the latter part of his campaign was held at the much larger Olympia Hall as the numbers grew and many manifestations and miracles took place.

It has been stated that Smith Wigglesworth raised 14 people from the dead, during the course of his ministry.

British Evangelist Smith Wigglesworth, preaching straight from the bible!
Public Domain: en.wikipedia.org/wiki/commons

Wigglesworth's ministry took him to the USA, Australia, New Zealand, South Africa, Sweden, Pacific Islands, India, Ceylon and several countries in Europe

Many such as my grandmother & great grandparents had the blessing and privilege of receiving from Evangelist Smith Wigglesworth's ministry.

Rev John Wilkinson my Spiritual father in the faith and ministry in the early years, also had the blessing and privilege of receiving from God, through this man of great faith.

Smith Wigglesworth (10th June 1859 to 12th March 1947)
Public Domain: healingandrevival.com

In 1904-1905 the Welsh Revival took place with Evan Roberts (8th June 1878 to 29th January 1951) as the leading figure.

He was a young man with no theological training, that spent hours and days in prayer privately and at public meetings.

He worked in the coal mines from the age of 11 years up until 23 years of age, assisting his father.

The Holy Spirit got hold of him at times, in such a way that many thought something was wrong with him.

Revivalist Evan Roberts (8th June 1878 to 29th January 1951) leader of the 1904-1905 Welsh Revival.
Public Domain: revival-library.org

He always carried his Bible with him in the mines. One day an explosion occurred scorching his Bible.

He had visitations from the Holy Spirit, showing all of Wales being lifted up to Heaven.

Then he came to the belief that God could save 100,000 souls. By October of 1904 there was more than 100,000 souls converted to Christ.

The Welsh Revival is believed to have triggered or at least played a part in at least 30 other revivals. India was one of those places and then from India to South Korea.

The Holy Spirit gave Evan Roberts four things that were a requirement at every revival meeting he conducted as follows:

1. Confession of all known sin. 2. Repentance and restitution. 3. Obedience and surrender to the Holy Spirit. 4. Public confession of Christ.

The Welsh Revival is also believed to have had a connection or relationship to The Asuza Street Revival.

William Joseph Seymour (1870-1922) the African American Revivalist that led the Asuza Street Revival.
Public Domain: en.wikipedia.org/wiki/commons

The primary leader of the Asuza Street Revival was African American evangelist William J. Seymour. He was the second of eight children born in Centreville, Louisiana, to emancipated slaves Simon Seymour and Phyllis Salabarr.

He was raised with Catholic and Baptist affiliations in extreme poverty in Louisiana and eventually came to Los Angeles from Mississippi, to preach the apostolic faith.

The revival meetings quickly grew to crowds of 1500 or more, packed into the small mission, at 312 Asuza Street, Los Angeles, California, for the best part of the 3 year period of the peak of the revival.

Men such as F.F Bosworth and Thomas Hezmalhalch, John G. Lake, Charles Parham and others attended the revival meetings and took what they received to their respective mission fields. William J Seymour, passed away at the age of 52 in Los Angeles, California.

Evangelist Charles F. Parham (June 4, 1873 –January 29, 1929)
Public Domain: william-branham.org

William had been a student of the early Pentecostal minister and Father of modern day Pentecostalism, Charles Fox Parham (June 4, 1873– January 29, 1929).

He adopted his teaching which combined the baptism of the Holy Spirit with speaking in tongues (glossolalia), such as was experienced in Jerusalem on the Day of Pentecost, as recorded in Acts chapter 2.

William & Charles eventually parted ways over disagreements concerning certain doctrines and racial tensions that existed in that day.

The Azusa Street Revival, beginning in the spring of 1906, largely spawned the worldwide Pentecostal movement. It commenced in a former African Methodist Episcopal Church which became the Apostolic Faith Gospel Mission (as shown in the following photo).

The Old African Methodist Episcopal Church Building at 312 Asuza Street, Los Angeles, where the Asuza Street Revival started in 1906.
Public Domain: en.m.wikipedia.org/commons

In 1908 Sarah Jane (nee Murrell) Lancaster (born 1858 in Williamstown Vic. Australia died 1939) purchased a former Temperance Hall shop front at 108 Queensbury Street, Nth Melbourne. The building became known as Good News Hall.

She conducted regular gospel healing meetings there and began to gather a congregation. Her ministry began with all-night prayer meetings and attendance rapidly grew to the capacity of the hall which seated 300.

In 1926 she aligned herself and the work to the Apostolic Faith Mission Australasia, which was an identification with Apostolic Faith Mission at Asuza Street, along with its Pentecostal doctrine and practice.

Temperance Hall (to the left) Purchased by Sarah Jane Lancaster in 1908. It was renamed Good News Hall and became the first Pentecostal Church in Australia.
Public Domain: Courtesy of Nth Melbourne Public Library

The following is a picture of Patrick's grandmother, a young Ruth (nee Lowe) O'Neal. She was one of nine children born to Ps Albert Lowe and Mrs Mary Lowe. She had the privilege of being in Sunday School when Smith Wigglesworth came to Melbourne, Australia during the early revival.

A young Ruth (nee Lowe) O'Neal. (Born 29th November 1922, called home 24th December 2015) Daughter of Ps Albert Lowe & Mrs Lowe. She was part of the Sunshine Revival that gave birth to Richmond Temple.
Credit: Patrick M. O'Neal (2006)

I thank God for those who sought the Lord and waited on Him, for the outpouring of his Holy Spirit! They prayed, they laboured, they called upon the Lord.

Many of us will never know the prayers prayed and the sacrifices made by those of the generations before us. What we have today along with the great spiritual legacy is something we must not take for granted.

She lived to see five generations of God's salvation and mercy to her family, up until her call home to glory on the 24th of December 2015!

Let us pray that God will do it again and again! We need a revival in our generation like never before.

The return of the Lord Jesus Christ is nearer than it has ever been. Will we be ready? Will He find faith on the earth when He returns?

Let us watch and pray and be about the Father's business of winning the lost and making disciples!

This gospel of the kingdom must continue to be preached in all the earth.

Luke 1:50 *"And His mercy is on those who fear Him from generation to generation."*

Let us pray for the sons and daughters of God that are to come!

***

2 TIMOTHY 1 : 3 - 7

*"³ I thank God, whom I serve with a pure conscience, as my forefathers did, as without ceasing I remember you in my prayers night and day, ⁴ greatly desiring to see you, being mindful of your tears, that I may be filled with joy, ⁵ **when I call to remembrance the genuine faith that is in you, which dwelt first in your grandmother Lois and your mother Eunice, and I am persuaded is in you also.** ⁶ Therefore I remind you to stir up the gift of God which is in you through the laying on of my hands. ⁷ For God has not given us a spirit of fear, but of power and of love and of a sound mind."*

***

ABOUT THE AUTHOR

Dr. Patrick M. O'Neal came to Christ in his teens, after his life had been miraculously spared three times, by the grace of God before he had reached the aged of 15. He has two younger brothers. The eldest of the two brothers went on to glory more than 30 years ago after a serious motor accident.

He is married and serves alongside his pastorally and prophetically gifted and ordained wife Diane, and has five children and 16 grandchildren. He has often been referred to over the years as one of those crazy Pentecostal Christians that never stops preaching the gospel. He is recognised as an apostle, as well as being prophetic and multi-faceted in ministry expression and gifting.

He struggled to accept and embrace His calling to apostolic ministry for many years, for various reasons. He finally accepted his call as an apostle nearly 25 years ago, through a series of divine interventions and confirmations.

The Lord Jesus spoke to him very clearly one day and said, *"I have called you as an apostle and I am now sending you to Africa to raise up sons"* Needless to say he used to pray *"Lord please don't send me to Africa"*. The rest is history. He ended up spending nearly six months of every year preaching, teaching, church planting and mentoring many leaders, churches and ministries in Africa.

He is a fourth-generation Pentecostal believer with several family members having gone before him, who have faithfully served in Christian ministry. His great-grandfather was one of the first ordained Pentecostal ministers in Australia and a key exponent of the 1926 Sunshine Revival which produced the former Richmond Temple as part of the early Pentecostal movement in Australia.

He has written several manuals which he circulates among those he mentors and those he oversees in the Heart Apostolic Ministries Int Network. He is the Founder and General Overseer along with his wife Diane and shares the leadership of H.A.M. Intl Network with the appointed overseers, operating in Australia, USA, Asia & Africa. Church planting, missions & leadership have always been part of his passion and focus in the kingdom of God.

He has been an ordained minister for the past 27 years and holds a Doctor of Divinity which he received in 2013 through TIC University USA. He did his earlier biblical and theological studies through I.C.I. in Brussels, Belgium and Harvest Bible College in Melbourne Australia, receiving a Diploma and a Bachelor's Degree in Biblical Studies with majors in church planting, leadership, Islam and missions.

His early years in ministry (which commenced more than 37 years ago) were spent working at Teen Challenge Vic. Australia in a teaching and counselling role, helping those who were drug and alcohol affected along with various other life-controlling problems. The many years he spent at Teen Challenge included much in-service training and study under the leadership of the late Rev Gordon Broussard.

Patrick and his wife Diane have many spiritual sons and daughters all over the globe. They are affectionately known as Dad and Mum, or Papa and Mama by many they mentor. They believe spiritual family relationships come before structure in the church and kingdom of God.

"Presence before performance", is one of Patrick's favourite sayings, learned through a severe period of *stress burn out* that he experienced in his Mid 20's!

He along with his wife Diane and others, travel widely and engage in missions, church planting, seminars, conferences, crusades, mentoring, counselling etc. He comes from an electrical engineering and electrical trades background along with multiple other secular qualifications.

He has an absolute passion and love for the Church and the kingdom of God! Your Kingdom come, Your will be done is his constant prayer!

Matthew 6:9-13

"Our Father in heaven, Hallowed be Your name.
[10] Your kingdom come. Your will be done on earth as it is in heaven.
[11] Give us this day our daily bread.
[12] And forgive us our debts, as we forgive our debtors.
[13] And do not lead us into temptation, But deliver us from the evil one.
For Yours is the kingdom and the power and the glory forever. Amen."

MAY YOU ALWAYS BE BLESSED IN HIM!

FUTURE PUBLICATIONS

BOOK TITLES TO LOOK OUT FOR IN THE FUTURE
by Dr Patrick M. O'Neal

'The Heart Prepared' - *Seen in Holiness and the Fear of the Lord*

'The Church' - *Principles, Patterns and Problems*

'The Life and Spirit of the Apostle'

'The Life and Spirit of the Prophet'

'The Holy Spirit' - *His Person, His Presence, His Work*

www.ingramcontent.com/pod-product-compliance
Lightning Source LLC
Chambersburg PA
CBHW050314010526
44107CB00055B/2242